Physical Characteristics of the Bichon Frise
(from The Kennel Club's Breed Standard)

BODY
Forechest well developed, deep brisket. Ribs well sprung, floating ribs not terminating abruptly. Loin broad, well muscled, slightly arched and well tucked up. Pelvis broad, croup slightly rounded. Length from withers to tailset should equal height from withers to ground.

HINDQUARTERS
Thighs broad and well rounded. Stifles well bent; hocks well angulated and metatarsals perpendicular.

TAIL
Normally carried raised and curled gracefully over the back but not tightly curled. Never docked.

COAT
Fine, silky with soft corkscrew curls. Neither flat nor corded, and measuring 7 to 10 cms (3 to 4 inches) in length. The dog may be presented untrimmed or have muzzle and feet slightly tidied up.

COLOUR
White, but cream or apricot markings acceptable up to 18 months of age. Under white coat, dark pigment desirable. Black, blue or beige markings often found on skin.

SIZE
Ideal height 23 to 28 cms (9 to 11 inches) at withers.

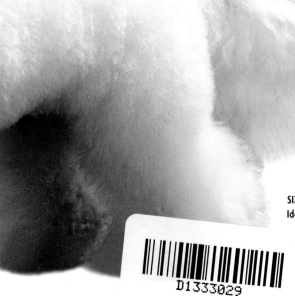

it, rounded and well knuckled up. Pads black. Nails :ferably black.

Bichon Frise

◇

by Juliette Cunliffe

Table of Contents

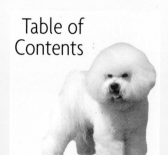

9

22

The History of the Bichon Frise

Consider the various theories of the evolution of the Bichon breeds and the spread of these fluffy little dogs around the world. Understand the origin of the Bichon Frise and how the breed was prized by the royals and common folk alike.

32

Characteristics of the Bichon Frise

Consider the many charming attributes of the Bichon Frise and determine whether you are an ideal owner of this exuberant companion dog. Learn about the breed's physical characteristics, including its coat and whiteness, as well as the breed's health considerations.

The Breed Standard for the Bichon Frise

Learn the requirements of a well-bred Bichon Frise by studying the description of the breed set forth in The Kennel Club standard. Both show dogs and pets must possess key characteristics as outlined in the breed standard.

38

64

Your Puppy Bichon Frise

Be advised about choosing a reputable breeder and selecting a healthy, typical puppy. Understand the responsibilities of ownership, including home preparation, acclimatization, the vet and prevention of common puppy problems.

DISTRIBUTED BY:

INTERPET
PUBLISHING

Vincent Lane, Dorking
Surrey RH4 3YX
England

ISBN 978-1-902389-20-2

Everyday Care of Your Bichon Frise

Enter into a sensible discussion of dietary and feeding considerations, exercise, grooming, travelling and identification of your dog. This chapter discusses Bichon Frise care for all stages of development.

Housebreaking and Training Your Bichon Frise

by Charlotte Schwartz
Be informed about the importance of training your Bichon Frise, from the basics of housebreaking, and understanding the development of a young dog, to executing obedience commands (sit, stay, down, etc.).

86

Health Care of Your Bichon Frise

Discover how to select a proper veterinary surgeon and care for your dog at all stages of life. Topics include vaccination scheduling, skin problems, dealing with external and internal parasites and the medical conditions common to the breed.

111

142

Your Senior Bichon Frise

Recognise the signs of an ageing dog, both behavioural and medical; implement a senior-care programme with your veterinary surgeon and become comfortable with making the final decisions and arrangements for your senior Bichon Frise.

149

Showing Your Bichon Frise

Experience the dog show world, including different types of shows and the making up of a champion. Go beyond the conformation ring to working trials and agility trials, etc.

Index: **156**

Copyright © 1999, **2008**
Kennel Club Books® A Division of BowTie, Inc.
Cover design patented: US 6,435,559 B2
Printed in South Korea

Theories about the origin of the Bichon Frise vary quite considerably, but the ancestor is generally accepted as being the French breed known as the Barbet, or Water Spaniel. From the Barbet came the name 'Barbichon,' which was later shortened to become 'Bichon.' The word 'Barbichon' probably evolved from the French word for beard, *barbiche*. All called 'Bichon' and originating in the Mediterranean region, four different categories of dog were acknowledged: the Bichon Maltais, Bichon Bolognaise, Bichon Havanais and Bichon Teneriffe, who later became known as the Bichon à Poil Frisé, and, subsequently, as the Bichon Frise we know today.

All of these dogs were appreciated for their disposition and character and were often used as goods with which to barter. So it was that these little dogs travelled widely, being transported from one continent to another by sailors.

Opposite page: The country of origin of the Bichon Frise is probably France. Sailors carried these little dogs around the world as barter and gifts, thus establishing varieties of Bichon-like dogs in different parts of the world.

THE BICHON IN SPAIN

Travelling from Eastern Mediterranean regions to the Balearic Islands, Teneriffe and the Canary Islands, it is usually accepted that it was sailors who introduced the Bichon to Teneriffe. The name of the island was used largely because it enhanced the commercial value of the dog, the very name 'Teneriffe' then sounding rather exotic.

The Bichon Teneriffe was particularly popular in Spanish

The Bichon was especially popular in 16th-century Spain among royalty and among artists, who often depicted the dogs in their work.

9

courts during the 16th century, and painters of the Spanish school often included such dogs in their paintings. Several can be found, particularly in the works of Goya (1746–1828). Goya was both a painter and an etcher and was taken on as court artist to Charles IV in 1789.

THE BICHON IN ITALY

Although known as far back as the 11th century, it was in the 14th century that the Bichon became a particular favourite of the nobility and, as with several other breeds of dog kept in Italy at that time, many were cut into lion trim. They became especially popular in the city of Bologna in northern Italy, and this has become the breed we now know as the Bolognese. However, in Britain this breed is much less well known than the Bichon Frise.

In early centuries, Bolognese were highly regarded for their excellent hearing and, although small in size, were often used as watch dogs. In the late 17th century, Bichons Bolognese were sent as gifts from Italian aristocrats to others in France and in Belgium, so spreading their wings still further.

Opposite page: The Bichon Bolognese, shown here, is the Italian Bichon variety.

THE BICHON IN FRANCE

Under Francis I (1515–1547), the Bichon, known as the Bichon Teneriffe, appeared in France and a few decades later became especially popular. It was in the court of Henry III (1547–1589) where this captivating little dog found

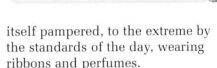

Did You Know?

These charming little dogs were tenderly cared for by their owners, and the French verb, *bichonner*, which directly translated means 'to doll up' or 'to pamper,' seems to have been evolved from them.

itself pampered, to the extreme by the standards of the day, wearing ribbons and perfumes.

It was recorded that the French kings and their ladies loved their little white dogs so much that they carried them with them everywhere, 'in traylike baskets attached around their necks by ribbons.' Under Louis XIV, who reigned from 1643 to 1715, the small dog was designated as the court 'pet of choice,' reputedly because it was easy to carry about.

Numerous French paintings depict dogs that were Bichon in type, and they also appear fre-

Bichon Frise

The fabled Bichon Havanese, which derived from the Blanquito de la Habana, is a close relative of the original Bichon Frise. The breed is recently featured in the book *Bichon Havanese* by Zoila Portuondo Guerra.

The famed Blanquito de la Habana derived from the original Spanish Bichon-type dogs and was the basis for the Bichon Havanais, a breed that is known for the silken texture of its coat.

quently in tapestries of earlier years, especially those woven in the 15th century. However, it would appear that from 1789, during the French Revolution, they were far less prominent, but they re-emerged with Napoleon III, who declared himself Emperor in 1852.

THE BICHON HAVANAIS

Theories as to the actual origin of the Bichon Havanais are many and varied. This is the breed known today as the Havanese, although, like the Bolognese, it is much less well known than its close relative the Bichon Frise.

12

It may be that the Bichon Havanais descended from the Bolognese and was taken to Argentina by Italians. There it could possibly have been crossed with a small South American Poodle, which effectively would have created another breed.

Another, perhaps more plausible theory, is that the Bichon Havanais instead descended from the Bichon Maltais. These Maltese, as we know them now, were taken to the West Indies by Spaniards. There they became known as the Blanquito de la Habana or Havana Silk Dog, the predecessor of the Havanese we know today.

Two other theories are also worthy of consideration. They may have arrived in Cuba during the time of Spanish colonisation and

A photograph of a Vicente Escobar painting that shows a young lady with a Blanquito de la Habana. Escobar was a famous Cuban portrait painter (1757-1854), and this is the earliest (and only) painting of this extinct breed. The original is in the archives of the Salas del Museo Nacional de Cuba in Havana, where it has not been on exhibit for many years.

exploration, or Italians may indeed have taken them to Cuba as gifts. Whatever their origin, the Bichons Havanais became much adored pets of wealthy Cubans. The Cubans gave these dogs as gifts and somehow they eventually found their way back to Europe.

Although the Bichon Frise we know today is a distinct breed, this has not always been the case. A review in a French magazine published in 1935 actually listed seven names as belonging to what was described as 'the same breed name as Bichon.' These were the Dog of Tenerife, the Dog of Havana, the Dog of Bologna, the Dog of the Baleares, the Dog of Peru, the Dog of Holland and the Little Lion Dog as described by Buffon, whose works were published in many volumes between 1755 and 1789.

Did You Know?

Early American breeders thought the Bichon should be included in the AKC's Non-Sporting Group (like The Kennel Club's Utility Group) rather than the Toy Group, considering that in substance, attitude and type it was better suited to the former. To this day, in the USA the Bichon remains in the Non-Sporting Group, rather than being included with Toys as is the case in Britain.

13

Bichon Frise

In considering look-alikes, the Poodle does have a fair resemblance to the Bichon Frise. It is possible that an early Bichon relative may have been crossed with a Poodle variety.

THE LITTLE LION DOG

Because it has been linked with the Bichon Frise in history it is also of interest to note the connection of the Little Lion Dog, known more familiarly as the Löwchen, or by the French name, Petit Chien Lion. The connection between the two is probably not close. The outlines of the two breeds are quite different in shape, and the coats are not similar. It is highly likely that there is some terrier blood in the Löwchen, and though there may be a little, it is certainly not found to this degree in any other of the truly Bichon breeds.

To confuse the issue, the now familiar 'lion trim' of the Löw-

The Löwchen, or Little Lion Dog, historically has been linked with both the Bichon Frise and the Bichon Havanais.

14

Reunion, but eventually the breed was to become extinct on the island.

Thankfully, somehow the Coton reappeared at Tulear on the southwestern coast of Madagascar. This was an active trading port and so, once again, the sailors had undoubtedly played their important part in moving another related breed to yet another country.

The Coton de Tulear's reappearance is a direct result of sailors' bartering Bichon-type dogs for goods, as the breed eventually ended up on the coast of Madagascar in the port of Tulear.

chen had been used on many other breeds of dog in the past, and this can only add to one's dilemma when trying to ascertain exactly which breeds were depicted in early representations.

THE COTON DE TULEAR

The little-known Coton de Tulear also cannot go without mention, for its history can be traced back to the Bichon Teneriffe. As trade routes opened up, the Bichon Teneriffe found its way to the island of Reunion in the Indian Ocean. It was here that this little Bichon developed a cotton-like coat, probably the result of a single genetic mutation. This dog was now known as the Coton de

THE BICHON'S DECLINE

Despite centuries of having been a pampered pet, towards the close of the 19th century the Bichon seemed to go out of fashion. The reason for this is not easy to comprehend, for in France prosperity was increasing. However, some

15

The Coton de Tulear bears much resemblance to the Bichon Frise.

were still to be found with circuses and fairs, often called 'the dog of the street' or sometimes 'little sheep dog.' Their lives were far removed from the luxury the breed had known in earlier years. Sometimes they could be found roaming the streets and were occasional companions to the blind.

THE BREED'S REVIVAL
When the First World War was behind them, a handful of breeders in France and Belgium decided to create a breeding programme for the Bichon Teneriffe, or Bichon à Poil Frisé. This, they

hoped, would revive the breed and take it beyond the status of the circus or street dog.

Enthusiasm amongst this small band of dedicated followers was such that by 1933 enough progress had been made for a breed standard to be drawn up. This was written by Mme Bouctovagniez, who was President of the Toy Club of France, aided by 'Friends of the Belgian Breeds.' However when the question of a breed name arose, it was Mme Nizet de Leemans, head of the Fédération Cynologique Internationale's (FCI's) Breed Standards Committee who made this important decision.

The story has been related that at a meeting in 1933 there was heated discussion about what the breed was to be called. In simple desperation, Mme Nizet de Leemans asked what the breed looked like. It was described as a fluffy little white dog, so she said, without more ado, that it was to be called Bichon Frise, meaning fluffy little dog. So it was that on October 18, 1934, the Bichon Frise was registered in the *Livre des Origines Francaises*. Despite this historical decision, many people continued to use the names Bichon Teneriffe or Bichon à Poil Frisé even into the early 1950s.

INBREEDING

In the years of the breed's revival there was only a limited supply of foundation stock, so it was understandable that inbreeding had to take place. Inbreeding we define as mating closely related dogs, such as mother to son or father to daughter. Amongst the early pioneers of the breed were M et Mme Bellotte, owners of the Milton prefix, and whose first registered Bichon Frise was born in 1929. To

The Bichon Maltais, more commonly known simply as the Maltese, is the predecessor of the Bichon Havanais and as well as one of today's most popular breeds.

You have to start with a good dog and give it a very professional grooming before it can be shown. Bichons Frises are recognised the world over for their beautiful and distinct white coats.

decades! The breed first became active in the USA in 1956 and it took 17 years for the Bichon Frise to obtain full American Kennel Club (AKC) recognition. To those unfamiliar with the official acceptance of 'new' breeds in America, 17 years may seem a very long time, but given the fragmented history of the Bichon, this is far from the case.

Although there were Bichons that arrived in America between the 1920s and 1940s, they had entered just as family pets of people who had travelled to Europe. For the purposes of official introduction to the country, events leading to the entry of the breed to the USA must therefore be said to have begun in 1952, when Helene and Francais Picault acquired their first Bichon in Dieppe, France. The couple's daughters married Americans, and in October 1956 M et Mme Picault and seven Bichons joined one of their daughters in Milwaukee, Wisconsin. Six months later two more

warrant registration, this dog must have been purebred for at least four generations.

THE BICHON FRISE IN THE USA

Considering that the Bichon had reached such depths of obscurity until its revival following the First World War, it has certainly come on in leaps and bounds in recent

Bichons followed them.

The Picaults had apparently been told that they would make a 'fortune' from breeding Bichons in the USA, but all was not as simple as it had been made to appear. Although the breed was thought charming, it was not registered and few puppies were sold in the early days following their arrival. Azelia Gascoigne of Wisconsin had already been involved with other breeds, and she bought her first Bichon in 1956, believing that the breed had potential. Another of the early Bichon purchasers was Mrs Fournier, who was a Collie breeder.

It took the Bichon awhile to gain popularity, just as it took Bichon fanciers time to learn the proper ways of grooming and coat care. The breed's image was improved greatly through increased attention to grooming and uniform presentation.

Although progress in bringing the breed to the notice of the public was slow, Mrs Fournier tried hard to promote the breed and advertised the Bichon in a national dog magazine. Finally, in May 1964, the formation of a national club was discussed at a meeting in San Diego, California. This was to be called the Bichon Frise Club of America, Mrs Gascoigne becoming the club's first President and Mrs Fournier its Registrar and Secretary.

Through the club, various local groups of Bichon enthusiasts were brought together and the possibility of getting the breed registered with the AKC was on everyone's lips. However, the

Bichon was not really taken seriously by other canine enthusiasts in the USA. Some Americans who had travelled to Europe had noticed the Bichon Frise in Continental dog shows, noting the lack of careful grooming and show presentation that seemed to plague the breed.

In 1969 top professional handler and Poodle man Frank Sabella visited an annual meeting of the breed club, giving his own ideas and suggestions as to how the breed's image could be improved by presentation. He demonstrated how to wash and blow-dry a Bichon, as well as the now important scissoring process and handling. Someone else who greatly helped to promote the new image of the breed was Richard Beauchamp, then editor of a leading dog magazine and today an international judge and author. He agreed to join others in the fight for breed recognition and undoubtedly in this he helped greatly.

The eventual outcome was that the Bichon Frise was accepted in the AKC's Miscellaneous Class in 1971 and entered into the AKC Stud Book in 1972, receiving full recognition in 1973.

The Bichon Frise was finally accepted in 1971, and then fully recognised in 1973, by the American Kennel Club. This occurred more than 100 years after its recognition as a specific breed in Europe.

THE BICHON IN BRITAIN

Even as late as the beginning of the 1970s, there were no Bichons known in Britain, although one kept as a pet had been registered with The Kennel Club in 1957. Even though this dog was not active in any other way, because of its registration the breed could be registered immediately upon arrival in the early 1970s.

The real beginning of the breed in Britain was in 1973 when Mr and Mrs J Sorstein from the USA came to live in Britain, bringing with them two Bichons Frises, a dog and a bitch.

The Sorteins' Bichons, Rava's Regal Valor of Reenroy and Jenny-Vive de Carlise, were bred together, and the first litter born in Britain was whelped in 1974. From this litter three puppies returned to the USA but two were shown in the UK. The dog, Carlise Cicero of Tresilva, was later to become an Australian champion. This same dog was the sire of Int Ch Tresilva Don Azur, who made an impact on the breed in Sweden. The mating was repeated in 1975, producing five puppies, helping to form the foundation of other Bichon kennels.

By the 1970s, undoubtedly the charming Bichon Frise had gained many admirers throughout the world and its fame spread. Since then, bloodlines have been exchanged from country to country thanks to numerous exports.

The first Bichon Frise, a pet dog, was registered with The Kennel Club in 1957. It is now a popular breed in the UK as both a companion and a show dog.

The breed is now most certainly one which is taken very seriously. Presentation is first-rate and many high accolades have been achieved, including Best in Show wins and first in the Toy Group at the prestigious Crufts Show in 1999.

21

Characteristics of the
BICHON FRISE

The Bichon Frise, though fairly small in stature, has a big personality and is great fun to own. Described as 'energy and affection in a powder-puff package,' this is a remarkably affectionate and intelligent breed with stylish good

eration when taking on a Bichon Frise.

A long-lived breed, the Bichon Frise can often live to 15 or 16 years of age, so this is another factor that must be seriously contemplated before deciding that

Once you have fallen in love with the Bichon Frise, you may be enamoured for life! Because the Bichon Frise is so small, intelligent, loveable and well behaved, it is easy to keep more than one. Who can resist?

looks. However, to keep the coat looking as good as it does in the pictures you will find in this book, a certain amount of time and dedication is needed. A coat kept in tip-top condition usually has attention paid to it every day, so this is a very important consid-

this is really the breed for you. Clearly, when taking a new pet into your home, the ultimate aim will be that the dog remains with you for life.

The Bichon has risen rapidly in the popularity stakes and currently there are 2000 to 3000 new puppies registered with The Kennel Club each year. This puts the breed in the top 20 most popular of all breeds registered in the UK. When one considers that in 1976 there were only 31 Bichon Frise puppies registered with The Kennel Club, the breed's rise to fame is little less than meteoric!

PHYSICAL CHARACTERISTICS

Because of the Bichon's profuse curly white coat, the physical structure concealed beneath can come as something of a surprise to the uninitiated. This is an exceptionally sound breed, not exaggerated structurally in any way. Although the Bichon is actually just a little longer than high, this is not immediately apparent because of the coat that stands off the body, creating an overall powder-puff appearance.

Thanks to the breed's sound construction, it is capable of moving with great ease, and many Bichons can be quite bouncy around the home. Bichons are quite capable of taking part in Mini-agility for they fall inside the height allowance, ideally measuring 23–28 cms (9–11 ins) to the top of the shoulder in the UK. In the USA the height can be up to 30.5 cms (12 ins).

No weight clause is specified in the standard for this breed, but weight usually falls somewhere between 4.5 and 8.25 kgs (10–18 lbs).

Apart from the coat, the head of the Bichon surely stands out as quite unforgettable, looking, as it does, like three lumps of coal on a background of snowy white. It is the grooming of the coat that creates the rounded appearance of the head, for underneath the furnishings the skull and muzzle shape are not at all extraordinary.

The head is set on a fairly long, arched neck, so that the head is carried high and proudly, conveying a thoroughly smart little dog with a big personality inside. The tail, too, gives an indication of the character of this little

Did You Know?

Face staining on the white Bichon is of genuine concern to many owners.

Sometimes staining can be caused by blocked tear ducts or ingrown eyelashes, but most of the time it is primarily a cosmetic problem. There are now many products available to remedy tear staining.

23

The standard describes the Bichon Frise as a 'gay, happy, lively little dog'...and that he is! Combine his wonderful personality with his stunning looks, and it's hard to think of a better choice for a pet.

one should settle for nothing less.'

A real extrovert, the Bichon is rarely shy or nervous and is a veritable joy to live with. He thrives on being the centre of attention. In history, this little dog has lived as a companion animal, and that is exactly what he should be for he appreciates all the comforts of home. A Bichon is happiest living in a home environment where he can take part in family life, and all the 'goings on' around him will be readily absorbed by his intelligent mind.

breed, for it is usually carried raised and curved gently over the back.

PERSONALITY

The Kennel Club's breed standard succinctly describes the breed as a 'gay, happy, lively little dog,' its temperament 'friendly and outgoing.' These few words speak volumes, but the American description of the breed's temperament is no less appealing, and warrants mention here: 'gentle mannered, sensitive, playful and affectionate. A cheerful attitude is the hallmark of the breed and

WHAT THE BICHON ENJOYS

The Bichon is a breed that enjoys training and learns well. Activities that he is capable of learning are obedience, therapy work, agility and even the odd trick or two. However, the Bichon does not take well to overly firm training and some seem to learn best when training takes the form of a little game. He is always ready to accept treats, so care must be taken that he does not inadvertently gain excess weight as a result of his training exercises.

When selecting collars and leads for training, chain collars should be avoided for they can too easily become entangled in the hair and may indeed damage the hair around the neck.

COLOUR AND COAT

Coat colour and coat presentation on the Bichon are very important, so owners of the breed must be prepared to put in a good deal of work to keep it in tip-top condition, never looking dirty or unkempt. A white coat will only stay white if bathed frequently.

The colour of the Bichon's coat is always white, but cream or apricot markings are acceptable up to 18 months of age. Under the white coat, the pigment should ideally be dark, and black, blue or beige markings can often be found on the skin.

The white of the coat contrasts strikingly against the black nose pigment and dark, round eyes with black pigment surrounding them. The skin that surrounds the eyes is usually black or dark grey. These areas are called haloes, and this dark skin colouring accentuates the eyes and enhances the expression of this delightful dog. Even the pads of the feet are black, and the nails should preferably be black too, although these are quite difficult

The Bichon Frise is much more than a lap dog. He thrives on exercise, running, jumping and playing games with his owner. As a matter of fact, sufficient exercise is necessary for his health.

to find.

Most Bichons are kept in a rather jaunty-looking trim, for this is how the breed is best known today, although this has not always been the case. Indeed it was the development of the breed's coat presentation that helped the Bichon to rise to fame. The coat style is undoubtedly one of the greatest attractions of the breed. Having said that, according to the English breed standard, the coat may be presented untrimmed, although I have to admit to never having seen an untrimmed Bichon in the show ring!

Coat texture is extremely important. The fine, silky coat has soft, corkscrew curls and is 7–10 cms (3–4 ins) in length. Although not mentioned in The Kennel Club's breed standard, the Bichon also has a soft, dense undercoat. For the show ring, the coat is trimmed to the natural outline of the body, rounded off and never cut so short as to create an overly trimmed or squared-off appearance. Pets are frequently kept with shorter coat on body and legs, but retaining the length on head, ears and tail to give a characteristic appearance.

The coat of the Bichon does not drop when it dies and is replaced, so as a result it must be combed out, otherwise knots and tangles will result. It is also very important in this breed that the coat is thoroughly groomed out before bathing; if not, the bathing procedure will only result in more tangles developing.

On the head, the beard and moustache are left longer, as are the ears, giving an overall rounded impression. The head coat is never trimmed so short that the breed loses its characteristic powder-puff appearance, and the coat on the tail, too, is left somewhat longer.

BICHONS WITH CHILDREN

Provided that parents have trained their children to treat dogs gently, being neither rough nor aggressive, most Bichons thoroughly enjoy playing with youngsters. It must, though, be understood that young children should always be supervised when in the company of dogs in order that accidents do not happen, however unintentional they might be.

BICHONS WITH OTHER FAMILY PETS

Always when one animal is introduced to another, careful supervision is essential. Most Bichons are quite prepared to associate with other animals, but a lot understandably depends on the personality of the other. An older dog or cat may not take readily to a newcomer to the household, although others accept them well. When a Bichon does find another canine or feline friend, usually the relationship is lasting and sincere. Indeed one of the dangers, in view of the Bichon's rather special coat, is mutual grooming that can play havoc with the coat, especially behind the ears!

Did You Know?

The easiest method of weighing your Bichon is on the bathroom scales. First weigh yourself alone, then a second time whilst holding the dog in your arms. Deduct one from the other to obtain the accurate weight of your Bichon. (This procedure inevitably encourages the owner's dieting as well... 'Is my subtraction really that rusty?'!)

Bichons Frises are, as a general rule, very healthy and happy pets. Newly acquired puppies should be examined by your veterinary surgeon to be sure that they are healthy, properly vaccinated and free of internal and external parasites.

HEALTH CONSIDERATIONS

In general this is a healthy, hardy little dog, but as in so many other breeds, certain health problems arise in the Bichon Frise. However, it is thanks to the dedication of breeders that these have been discovered. If owners are aware of the problems that can occur, they are undoubtedly in a position to deal with them in the best manner possible. Some problems are

Did You Know?

To take a urine sample to your veterinary surgeon for analysis, the easiest way is to catch the urine in a large, clean bowl and then transfer this to a bottle. Owners who have spent many fruitless hours attempting to get their dogs or bitches to urinate directly into a bottle will be yellow with envy to discover this little trick.

Bichon Frise

genetic and are carried via heredity, but others are not.

SKIN ALLERGIES

Some Bichons are prone to skin allergies, but they can often be kept under control with a carefully considered diet. The allergy is often noticed as 'hot spots' on the skin, despite there being no sign of external parasites. A low-protein diet often seems to suit skin troubles.

It is often extremely difficult to ascertain the cause of the allergy. There are many possibilities, ranging from the sitting room carpet, the shampoo used when bathing and, quite frequently, certain grasses and moulds. In cases of skin allergy, it is a good idea to change shampoo, conditioning rinse and any other coat sprays used, for these are perhaps the easiest items to eliminate before looking further if necessary. It goes without saying that your Bichon must be kept free of external parasites such as fleas.

LEG PROBLEMS

Bichons are known to suffer from trouble with the knee joints, known as luxating patella, though of course only a few are affected. A luxated patella simply means a 'slipped kneecap.' Reliable breeders have their breeding stock checked regularly by a vet, which has helped to reduce the incidence. Another important factor is that a dog should not be overweight as this is likely to exacerbate the problem.

Many dogs with luxating patella live with the problem without experiencing pain, but surgery is necessary in some cases.

Another problem currently being investigated in Bichons is one affecting the hip joint. Hip dysplasia, the most common of all canine orthopaedic problems, does not have a high incidence in the Bichon.

BLADDER STONES

Although found infrequently in the Bichon, bladder stones can sometimes cause a problem, as they are found more often in small breeds than in larger ones. Symptoms include frequent passing of urine, blood in the urine, straining to pass water, general weakness, depression and loss of appetite. Bladder stones occur more frequently in females than males.

Urgent veterinary attention is necessary, for stones in the bladder can lead to irreparable kidney damage and life can be lost as a result. In many cases stones can be dissolved by special diet under veterinary supervision, but certain types require surgical removal.

TEETH

As with many of the smaller breeds, some Bichons lose their teeth at a relatively early age. It is therefore important to pay close attention to the care of teeth and gums so that they remain as healthy as possible, thereby preventing decay, infec-

Puppy teeth are fine and sharp. You can start a dental care routine with your Bichon when he is a pup.

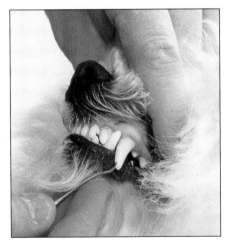

The adult Bichon Frise has larger, stronger teeth than the puppy.

tion and resultant loss.

Infection in the gums may not just stop there. The bacteria from this infection is carried through the bloodstream, the result of which can be disease of liver, kidney, heart, and the joints. This is all the more reason to realise that efficient dental care is of utmost importance throughout a dog's life.

Did You Know?

At the first sign of any minor infection, the author has often found that live yoghurt, administered orally, is of great benefit. This sometimes has the effect of rectifying the problem almost immediately, before a course of antibiotics becomes necessary.

29

EYES

A problem that has only recently been revealed in the Bichon Frise is that of cataracts, and the mode of inheritance is currently being researched. At this early stage of discovery, various schemes are currently implemented in different countries. It is therefore advisable for new owners to make enquiries as to whether or not tests are yet available in their own country.

Initially it would be sensible

Because the Bichon Frise's coat is such an important part of the dog's appearance, daily attention to tear stains is mandatory. Pet shops have specially made cosmetics and cleaners for tear stain removal.

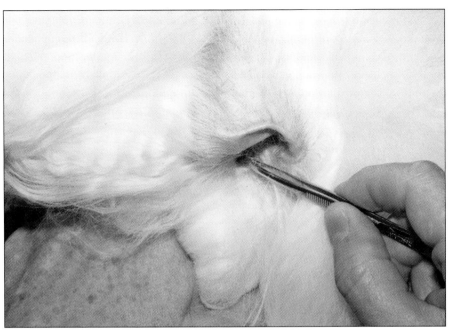

Excess hair growing in the dog's ear canal should be plucked out. With instruction and practice on your part, this can be a painless procedure for the dog.

to contact the secretary of a breed club to ascertain the current situation and obtain up-to-date information. Details of secretaries can be obtained from The Kennel Club.

Because of the hair around the eye of the Bichon, the eyeball can be irritated. This can result in conjunctivitis and is very likely to cause an excess of tear production. This, in consequence, causes tear staining below the eye, something often noticed on white and light-coloured dogs. Clearly, attention is therefore necessary to keep the eyes clean and this should be a routine aspect of grooming this breed.

EARS

Because the Bichon's ears hang close to the head and are well covered with flowing hair in accordance with the breed standard, there can be lack of ventilation. It is therefore important that ears are checked regularly and that excess hair is carefully plucked from inside the ear to avoid infection arising.

Signs of an infected ear include a brown odorous discharge that leads to the ear becoming red, inflamed and sore. At this stage the dog will scratch at the ear and may hold its head on one side because of the pain.

31

The Kennel Club breed standard for the Bichon Frise is effectively a 'blue-print' for the breed. It sets down the various points of the dog in words, enabling a visual picture to be conjured up in the mind of the reader. However, this is more easily said than done. Not only do standards vary from country to country, but people's interpretations of breed standards vary also. It is this difference of interpretation which makes judges select different dogs for top honours, for their opinions differ as to which dog most closely fits the breed standard. That is not to say that a good dog does not win regularly under different judges, nor that an inferior dog may rarely even be placed at a show, at least not amongst quality competition.

The breed standard given here is that authorised by The Kennel Club. It is very comprehensive compared with the standards of many other breeds, and so is reasonably self-explanatory. However, as with most breeds there are variances between the standard used in Britain and that in the USA. Notably, the English standard makes no mention of undercoat, but the Bichon Frise most certainly does have an undercoat, unlike its white-coated cousin, the Maltese. The American Kennel Club's standard tells readers that the undercoat is soft and dense, the outercoat of a coarser and curlier texture.

Another qualification in the American standard, worthy of mention, is the clause that 'Any colour in excess of 10% of the entire coat of a mature specimen is a fault and should be penalised...'. In Britain the standard only accepts such markings up to 18 months of age.

THE KENNEL CLUB STANDARD FOR THE BICHON FRISE

General Appearance: Well balanced dog of smart appearance, closely coated with handsome plume carried over the back. Natural white coat curling loosely. Head carriage proud and high.

Characteristics: Gay, happy, lively little dog.

Temperament: Friendly and outgoing.

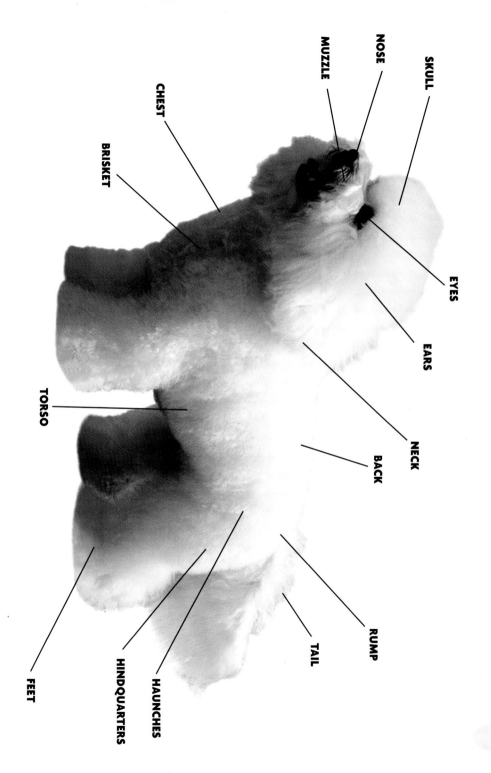

MUZZLE

NOSE

SKULL

CHEST

BRISKET

EYES

EARS

TORSO

NECK

BACK

RUMP

TAIL

FEET

HINDQUARTERS

HAUNCHES

33

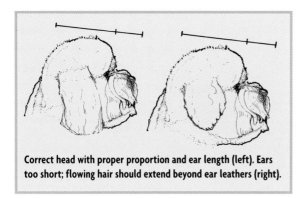

Correct head with proper proportion and ear length (left). Ears too short; flowing hair should extend beyond ear leathers (right).

Head and Skull: Ratio of muzzle length to skull length 3 : 5. On a head of the correct width and length, lines drawn between the outer corners of the eyes and nose will create a near equilateral triangle. Whole head in balance with body. Muzzle not thick, heavy or snipey. Cheeks flat, not very strongly muscled. Stop moderate but definite, hollow between eyebrows just visible. Skull slightly rounded, not coarse, with hair accentuating rounded appearance. Nose large, round, black, soft and shiny.

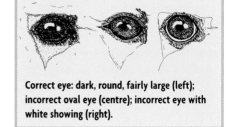

Correct eye: dark, round, fairly large (left); incorrect oval eye (centre); incorrect eye with white showing (right).

Eyes: Dark, round with black eye rims, surrounded by dark haloes, consisting of well pigmented skin. Forward-looking, fairly large but not almond-shaped, neither obliquely set nor protruding. Showing no white when looking forward. Alert, full of expression.

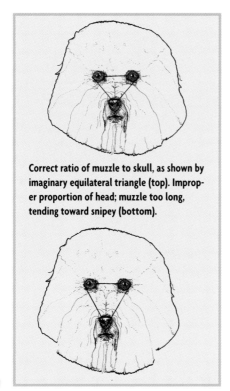

Correct ratio of muzzle to skull, as shown by imaginary equilateral triangle (top). Improper proportion of head; muzzle too long, tending toward snipey (bottom).

Ears: Hanging close to head, well covered with long flowing hair longer than leathers, set on slightly higher than eye level and rather forward on skull. Carried forward when dog alert, forward edge touching skull. Leather reaching approximately half-way along muzzle.

Mouth: Jaws strong, with a perfect, regular and complete scissor bite, i.e., upper teeth closely overlapping lower teeth and set square to the jaws. Full dentition desirable. Lips fine, fairly tight and completely black.

Neck: Arched neck fairly long, about one-third the length of body. Carried high and proudly. Round and slim near head, gradually broadening to fit smoothly into shoulders.

Forequarters: Shoulders oblique, not prominent, equal in length to upper arm. Upper arm fits close to body. Legs straight, perpendicular, when seen from front; not too finely boned. Pasterns short and straight viewed from front, very slightly sloping viewed from side.

Body: Forechest well developed, deep brisket. Ribs well sprung, floating ribs not terminating abruptly. Loin broad, well muscled, slightly arched and well tucked up. Pelvis broad, croup slightly rounded. Length from withers to tailset should equal height from withers to ground.

Hindquarters: Thighs broad and well rounded. Stifles well bent; hocks well angulated and metatarsals perpendicular.

Feet: Tight, rounded and well knuckled up. Pads black. Nails preferably black.

Tail: Normally carried raised and curved gracefully over the back but not tightly curled. Never docked. Carried in line with backbone, only hair touching back; tail itself not in contact. Set on level with topline, neither too high nor too low. Corkscrew tail undesirable.

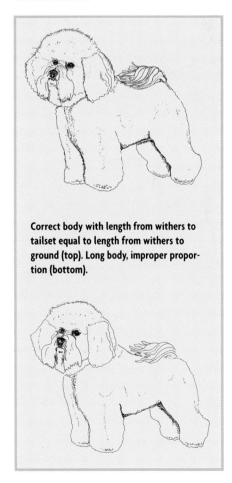

Correct body with length from withers to tailset equal to length from withers to ground (top). Long body, improper proportion (bottom).

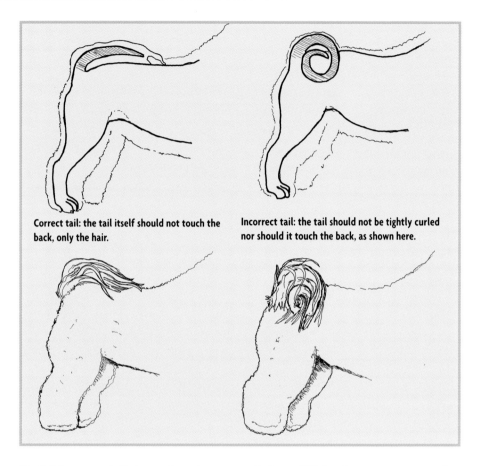

Correct tail: the tail itself should not touch the back, only the hair.

Incorrect tail: the tail should not be tightly curled nor should it touch the back, as shown here.

Gait/Movement: Balanced and effortless with an easy reach and drive maintaining a steady and level topline. Legs moving straight along line of travel, with hind pads showing.

Coat: Fine, silky and with soft corkscrew curls. Neither flat nor corded, and measuring 7–10 cms (3–4 ins) in length. The dog may be presented untrimmed or have muzzle and feet slightly tidied up.

Colour: White, but cream or apricot markings acceptable up to 18 months. Under white coat, dark pigment desirable. Black, blue or beige markings often found on skin.

Size: Ideal height 23–28 cms (9–11 ins) at withers.

Faults: Any departure from the foregoing points should be considered a fault and the seriousness with which the fault should be regarded should be in exact proportion to its degree.

Note: Male animals should have two apparently normal testicles fully descended into the scrotum.

Although a great deal can be learned from the breed standard, only by seeing good quality, typical specimens can one really learn to appreciate the breed's merits. Therefore readers interested in showing their Bichons should watch other dogs being exhibited, and learn as much as possible from established breeders and exhibitors.

It is sensible to attend specialist breed seminars, often hosted by breed clubs. Here the finer points of the breed can be explained fully and discussed. There is usually a dog, or perhaps several, available for demonstration purposes, and there may even be an opportunity for participants to feel beneath the coat for the structure of the animal.

Just a few elaborations on the breed standard are, however, worthy of brief comment.

Because correct pigmentation is so important for the Bichon, the eye rims should, as the standard states, be black. If pigment is broken up, or light, this completely changes the expression. We are told that the eyes are to be round, not almond in shape. If the eye is

of correct shape, the white of the eye will not show when the dog is looking in a forward direction.

Trimming and skilful artistic presentation can hide a multitude of shortcomings on coated breeds, especially the Bichon. The standard states quite clearly the correct set on and carriage of the ears, as well as their length. Good judges will always take care that presentation has not superficially remedied structural faults.

It should be noted that full dentition is desirable, although in Britain most judges do not count pre-molar and molar teeth in this breed, as is the case in several countries. There should be six upper and six lower incisors set between the canine teeth. The completely black lips are fine and fairly tight. They should never droop as this would alter the expression.

Height is measured from withers to ground, and this should be equal to the distance from withers to root of tail. There is a slight arch over the loin in the construction of the Bichon.

The Bichon is a sound little dog, and thus should it remain. Both breeders and judges should always be aware of structural faults that may not be apparent to the eye because of an expertly presented coat. Conversely, it must also be borne in mind that the appearance of a well-constructed dog can be ruined by poor presentation.

BICHON FRISE

You have probably decided on a Bichon Frise as your choice of pet following a visit to the home of a friend or acquaintance, where you have seen an adorable Bichon looking clean, pretty, and wandering happily around the house joining politely in the family fun. However, as a new owner you must realise that a good deal of care, commitment and careful training goes into raising a bois-terous puppy so that your pet turns into a well-behaved adult.

In deciding to take on a new · puppy, you will be committing yourself to around 15 years of responsibility. No dog should be discarded after a few months, or even a few years, after the novelty has worn off. Instead, your Bichon should be joining your household to spend the rest of its days with you.

This young Bichon shows his owner a little 'puppy love.' The Bichon Frise is known as being one of the most affectionate breeds around.

Although temperamentally a Bichon Frise is much easier to look after than many other breeds, you will still need to carry out a certain amount of training. Unlike some of the larger, guarding breeds, it will not respond well to overly strict training. Instead you will need to take a firm but gentle approach in order to get the very best out of your pet.

A Bichon generally likes to be clean around the house, but you will need to teach your puppy what is and is not expected. You will need to be consistent in your instructions; it is no good accepting certain behaviour one day and not the next. Not only will your puppy simply not understand, he will be utterly confused. Your Bichon will want to please you, so you will need to demonstrate clearly how your puppy is to achieve this.

Before making your commit-

ment to a new puppy, do also think carefully about your future holiday plans. If you have thought things through carefully, discussed the matter thoroughly with all the close members of your family, hopefully you will have come to the right decision. If you decide that a Bichon should join your

Did You Know?

Unfortunately, when a puppy is bought by someone who does not take into consideration the time and attention that dog ownership requires, it is the puppy who suffers when he is either abandoned or placed in a shelter by a frustrated owner. So all of the 'homework' you do in preparation for your pup's arrival will benefit you both. The more informed you are, the more you will know what to expect and the better equipped you will be to handle the ups and downs of raising a puppy. Hopefully, everyone in the household is willing to do his part in raising and caring for the pup. The anticipation of owning a dog often brings a lot of promises from excited family members: 'I will walk him every day,' 'I will feed him,' 'I will housebreak him,' etc., but these things take time and effort, and promises can easily be forgotten once the novelty of the new pet has worn off.

Puppies of all breeds need to chew, and one should not underestimate puppy teeth. Although small, puppy teeth are very sharp. Pups should be given strong, safe chew devices made especially for dogs.

You should select a Bichon puppy that comes from healthy parents and responsible breeding. The breeder will keep the pups with their dam for about eight weeks to ensure proper nourishment and socialisation among the litter.

Did You Know?

You should not even think about buying a puppy that looks sick, undernourished, overly frightened or nervous. Sometimes a timid puppy will warm up to you after a 30-minute 'let's-get-acquainted' session.

family this will hopefully be a happy, long-term relationship for all parties concerned.

BUYING A BICHON FRISE PUPPY

Although you may be looking for a Bichon as a pet, rather than a show dog, this does not mean that you want a dog that is in any way 'second-rate.' A caring breeder will have brought up the entire litter of puppies with the same amount of dedication, and a puppy destined for a pet home should be just as healthy as one that hopes to end up in the show ring.

Because you have carefully selected this breed, you will want a Bichon Frise that is a typical specimen, both in looks and temperament. In your endeavours to find such a puppy you will have to select the breeder with care. The Kennel Club will be able to give you names of contacts within Bichon breed clubs. These people can possibly put you in touch with breeders who may have puppies for sale. However, although they can point you in the right direction, it will be up to you to do your homework.

For potential buyers, it is a good idea to visit a show so that you can see quality specimens of the breed. This will also give you

Did You Know?

Your selection of a good puppy can be determined by your needs. A show potential or a good pet? It is your choice. Every puppy, however, should be of good temperament. Although show-quality puppies are bred and raised with emphasis on physical conformation, responsible breeders strive for equally good temperament. Do not buy from a breeder who concentrates solely on physical beauty at the expense of personality.

40

At eight weeks of age the puppies should be fully weaned and fairly well socialised with each other, and probably will have met some people other than the breeder. Their individual personalities will be evident by this time as well.

an opportunity to meet breeders who will probably be able to answer some of your queries. In addition, you will get some idea about which breeders appear to take most care of their stock, and which are likely to have given their puppies the best possible start in life.

When buying your puppy, you will need to know about vaccinations, those already given and those still due. It is important that any injections already given by a

Did You Know?

Your puppy should have a well-fed appearance but not a distended abdomen, which may indicate worms or incorrect feeding, or both. The body should be firm, with a solid feel. The skin of the abdomen should be pale pink and clean, without signs of scratching or rash. Check the hind legs to make certain that dewclaws were removed, if any were present at birth.

41

Three puppies eagerly await your attention, but the fourth has found something more interesting. Which kind of dog do you want? You'll probably find that the puppy chooses you much in the same way that you choose him!

veterinary surgeon have documentation to prove this. A worming routine is also vital for any young puppy, so the breeder should be able to tell you exactly what treatment has been given, when it has been administered, and how you should continue.

Clearly when selecting a

Documentation

Two important documents you will get from the breeder are the pup's pedigree and registration papers. The breeder should register the litter and each pup with The Kennel Club, and it is necessary for you to have the paperwork if you plan on showing or breeding in the future.

Make sure you know the breeder's intentions on which type of registration he will obtain for the pup. There are limited registrations which may prohibit the dog from being shown or from competing in non-conformation trials such as Working or Agility if the breeder feels that the pup is not of sufficient quality to do so. There is also a type of registration that will permit the dog in non-conformation competition only.

If your dog is registered with a Kennel-Club-recognised breed club, then you can register the pup with The Kennel Club yourself. Your breeder can assist you with the specifics of the registration process.

puppy, the one you choose must be in good condition. The coat should look healthy and there should be no discharge from eyes or nose. Ears should also be clean, and of course there should be absolutely no sign of parasites. Check that there is no rash on the skin, and of course the puppy you choose should not have evidence of loose motions.

As in several other breeds, a few Bichon Frise puppies have umbilical hernias, which can be a seen as a small lump on the tummy where the umbilical cord was attached. Clearly it is preferable not to have such a hernia on any puppy, but you should check for this at the outset and if there is one you should discuss the seriousness of this with the breeder. Most umbilical hernias are safe, but your vet should keep an eye on this in case an operation is warranted.

When buying a pup, always insist that you see the puppy's dam and, if possible, the sire. However, frequently the sire will not be owned by the breeder of the litter, but a photograph may be available for you to see. Ask if the breeder has any other of the puppy's relations that you could meet. For example, there may be an older half-sister or -brother and it would be interesting for you to see how he/she has turned out, the eventual size, coat quality, temperament and so on.

Be sure, too, that if you decide to buy a puppy, all relevant documentation is provided at the time of sale. You will need a copy of the pedigree, preferably Kennel Club registration documents, vaccination certificates and a feeding

chart so that you know exactly how the puppy has been fed and how you should continue. Some careful breeders provide their puppy buyers with a small amount of food. This prevents the risk of an upset tummy, allowing for a gradual change of diet if that particular brand of food is not locally available.

COMMITMENT OF OWNERSHIP
After considering all of these factors, you have most likely already made some very important decisions about selecting your puppy. You have chosen a Bichon Frise, which means that you have decided which characteristics you want in a dog and what type of dog will best fit into your family and lifestyle. If you have selected a breeder, you have gone a step further—you have done your

You should not feed your adult dog and puppy the same diet, as their nutritional needs are different. Feed each Bichon his own food from his own bowl.

Did You Know?

Breeders rarely release puppies until they are eight to ten weeks of age. This is an acceptable age for most breeds of dog, excepting toy breeds, which are not released until around 12 weeks, given their petite sizes. If a breeder has a puppy that is 12 weeks or more, it is likely well socialised and housetrained. Be sure that it is otherwise healthy before deciding to take it home.

research and found a responsible, conscientious person who breeds quality Bichons Frises and who should be a reliable source of help as you and your puppy adjust to life together. If you have observed a litter in action, you have obtained a firsthand look at the dynamics of a puppy 'pack' and, thus, you should learn about each pup's individual personality—perhaps you have even found one that particularly appeals to you.

However, even if you have not yet found the Bichon Frise puppy of your dreams, observing pups will help you learn to recognise certain behaviour and to determine what a pup's behaviour indicates about his temperament. You will be able to pick out which pups are the leaders, which ones are less outgoing, which ones are confident, which ones are shy, playful, friendly, aggressive, etc.

Your Schedule . . .

If you lead an erratic, unpredictable life, with daily or weekly changes in your work requirements, consider the problems of owning a puppy. The new puppy has to be fed regularly, socialised (loved, petted, handled, introduced to other people) and, most importantly, allowed to visit outdoors for toilet training. As the dog gets older, it can be more tolerant of deviations in its feeding and toilet relief.

Equally as important, you will learn to recognise what a healthy pup should look and act like. All of these things will help you in your search, and when you find the Bichon Frise that was meant for you, you will know it!

Researching your breed, selecting a responsible breeder and observing as many pups as possible are all important steps on the way to dog ownership. It may seem like a lot of effort...and you have not even taken the pup home yet! Remember, though, you cannot be too careful when it comes to deciding on the type of dog you want and finding out about your prospective pup's background. Buying a puppy is not—or should not be—just another whimsical purchase. This is one instance in which you actually do get to choose your own family! You may be thinking that buying a puppy should be fun—it should not be so serious and so much work. Keep in mind that your puppy is not a cuddly stuffed toy or decorative lawn ornament, but a creature that will become a real member of your family. You will come to realise that, whilst buying a puppy is a pleasurable and exciting endeavour, it is not something to be taken lightly. Relax...the fun will start when the pup comes home!

Always keep in mind that a puppy is nothing more than a baby in a furry disguise...a baby who is virtually helpless in a human world and who trusts his owner for fulfilment of his basic needs for survival. In addition to water and shelter, your pup needs care, protection, guidance and love. If you are not prepared to commit to this, then you are not prepared to own a dog.

Wait a minute, you say. How hard could this be? All of my neighbours own dogs and they seem to be doing just fine. Why should I have to worry about all of this? Well, you should not worry about it; in fact, you will probably find that once your Bichon Frise pup gets used to his new home, he will fall into his place in the family quite naturally. But it never hurts to emphasise the commitment of dog ownership. With some time and patience, it is really not too difficult to raise a curious and exuberant Bichon Frise pup to be a well-adjusted and well-mannered adult dog—a dog that could be your most loyal friend.

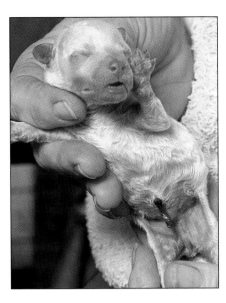

A new-born Bichon Frise, only a few minutes old.

Are You a Fit Owner?

If the breeder from whom you are buying a puppy asks you a lot of personal questions, do not be insulted. Such a breeder wants to be sure that you will be a fit provider for his puppy.

PREPARING PUPPY'S PLACE IN YOUR HOME

Researching your breed and finding a breeder are only two aspects of the 'homework' you will have to do before bringing your Bichon Frise puppy home. You will also have to prepare your home and family for the new addition. Much as you would prepare a nursery for a new-born baby, you will need to designate a place in your home that will be the puppy's own. How you prepare your home will depend on how much freedom the dog will be allowed. Whatever you decide, you must ensure that he has a place that he can 'call his own.'

When you bring your new puppy into your home, you are bringing him into what will become his home as well. Obviously, you did not buy a puppy so that he could take over your house, but in order for a puppy to grow into a stable, well-adjusted dog, he has to feel comfortable in his surroundings. Remember, he is leaving the warmth and security of his mother and littermates, as well as the familiarity of the only place he has ever known, so it is important to make his transition as easy as possible. By preparing a place in your home for the puppy, you are making him feel as welcome as possible in a strange new place. It should not take him long to get used to it, but the sudden shock of being transplanted is somewhat traumatic for a young pup. Imagine how a small child would feel in the same situation—that is how your puppy must be feeling. It is up to you to reassure

Most Bichons Frises quickly adapt to their crates.

Male or Female?

An important consideration to be discussed is the sex of your puppy. For a family companion, a bitch may be the better choice, considering the female's inbred concern for all young creatures and her accompanying tolerance and patience. It is always advised to spay a pet bitch, which may guarantee her a longer life.

him and to let him know, 'Little fellow, you are going to like it here!'

WHAT YOU SHOULD BUY
CRATE
To someone unfamiliar with the use of crates in dog training, it may seem like punishment to shut a dog in a crate, but this is not the case at all. Although all breeders

Insurance

Many good breeders will offer you insurance with your new puppy, which is an excellent idea. The first few weeks of insurance will probably be covered free of charge or with only minimal cost, allowing you to take up the policy when this expires. If you own a pet dog, it is sensible to take out such a policy as veterinary fees can be high, although routine vaccinations and boosters are not covered. Look carefully at the many options open to you before deciding which suits best.

do not advocate crate training, more and more breeders and trainers are recommending crates as a preferred tool for show puppies as well as pet puppies. Crates are not cruel—crates have many humane and highly effective uses in dog care and training. For example, crate training is a very popular and very successful housebreaking method. A crate can keep your dog safe during travel and, perhaps most importantly, a crate provides your dog with a place of his own in your home. It serves as a 'doggie bedroom' of sorts—your Bichon Frise can curl up in his crate when he wants to sleep or when he just needs a break. Many dogs sleep in their crates overnight. When lined with soft bedding and his favourite toy a crate becomes a

Your local pet shop should carry a complete assortment of crates and kennels. Get one large enough for the fully grown Bichon Frise.

PHOTO COURTESY OF DOSKOCIL

Did You Know?

Taking your dog from the breeder to your home in a car can be a very uncomfortable experience for both of you. The puppy will have been taken from his warm, friendly, safe environment and brought into a strange new environment. An environment that moves! Be prepared for loose bowels, urination, crying, whining and even fear biting. With proper love and encouragement when you arrive home, the stress of the trip should quickly disappear.

cosy pseudo-den for your dog. Like his ancestors, he too will seek out the comfort and retreat of a den—you just happen to be providing him with something a little more luxurious than his early ancestors enjoyed.

As far as purchasing a crate, the type that you buy is up to you. It will most likely be one of the two most popular types: wire or fibreglass. There are advantages and disadvantages to each type. For example, a wire crate is more open, allowing the air to flow through and affording the dog a view of what is going on around

47

The crate you select should be large enough so that your Bichon Frise can comfortably stand, turn around and lie down when he is fully grown.

medium-small crate will be necessary for a full-grown Bichon Frise, who stands approximately 11 inches high.

BEDDING

Veterinary bedding in the dog's crate will help the dog feel more at home and you may also like to pop in a small blanket. This will take the place of the leaves, twigs, etc., that the pup would use in the wild to make a den; the pup can make his own 'burrow' in the crate. Although your pup is far

him whilst a fibreglass crate is sturdier. Both can double as travel crates, providing protection for the dog. The size of the crate is another thing to consider. Puppies do not stay puppies forever—in fact, sometimes it seems as if they grow right before your eyes. A

Did You Know?

It will take at least two weeks for your puppy to become accustomed to his new surroundings. Give him lots of love, attention, handling, frequent opportunities to relieve himself, a diet he likes to eat and a place he can call his own.

Crate Training

During crate training, you should partition off the section of the crate in which the pup stays. If he is given too big an area, this will hinder your training efforts. Crate training is based on the fact that a dog does not like to soil his sleeping quarters, so it is ineffective to keep a pup in a crate that is so big that he can eliminate in one end and get far enough away from it to sleep. Also, you want to make the crate den-like for the pup. Blankets and a favourite toy will make the crate cosy for the small pup; as he grows, you may want to remove a blanket or two.

It will take some coaxing at first, but be patient. Given some time to get used to it, your pup will adapt to his new home-within-a-home quite nicely.

PHOTO COURTESY OF MIKKI PET PRODUCTS.

Pet shops offer a wide selection of suitable dog toys that your Bichon Frise will welcome. Never offer your dog toys that are manufactured for children as they may be dangerous to a teething puppy.

removed from his den-making ancestors, the denning instinct is still a part of his genetic makeup.

Second, until you bring your pup home, he has been sleeping amidst the warmth of his mother and littermates, and whilst a blanket is not the same as a warm, breathing body, it still provides heat and something with which to snuggle. You will want to wash your pup's bedding frequently in case he has an accident in his crate, and replace or remove any blanket that becomes ragged and starts to fall apart.

TOYS

Toys are a must for dogs of all ages, especially for curious playful pups. Puppies are the 'children' of the dog world, and what child

The crate can serve as the Bichon Frise's bedroom. Just leave the door open— once used to it, your Bichon wil go into his crate to rest without being told.

49

does not love toys? Chew toys provide enjoyment to both dog and owner—your dog will enjoy playing with his favourite toys, whilst you will enjoy the fact that they distract him from your expensive shoes and leather sofa. Puppies love to chew; in fact, chewing is a physical need for pups as they are teething, and everything looks appetising! The full range of your possessions—from old dishcloth to Oriental rug—are fair game in the eyes of a teething pup. Puppies are not all that discerning when it comes to finding something to literally 'sink their teeth into'—everything tastes great!

not for free play. If a pup 'disembowels' one of these, the small plastic squeaker inside can be dangerous if swallowed. Monitor the condition of all your pup's toys carefully and get rid of any that have been chewed to the point of becoming potentially dangerous.

Breeders advise owners to resist stuffed toys, because they can become de-stuffed in no time. The overly excited pup may ingest the stuffing, which is neither digestible nor nutritious.

Similarly, squeaky toys are quite popular, but must be avoided for the Bichon Frise. Perhaps a squeaky toy can be used as an aid in training, but

Toys, Toys, Toys

With a big variety of dog toys available, and so many that look like they would be a lot of fun for a dog, be careful in your selection. It is amazing what a set of puppy teeth can do to an innocent-looking toy, so, obviously, safety is a major consideration. Be sure to choose the most durable products that you can find. Hard nylon bones and toys are a safe bet, and many of them are offered in different scents and flavours that will be sure to capture your dog's attention. It is always fun to play a game of catch with your dog, and there are balls and flying discs that are specially made to withstand dog teeth.

Be careful of natural bones, which have a tendency to splinter into sharp, dangerous pieces. Also be careful of rawhide, which can turn into pieces that are easy to swallow or into a mushy mess on your carpet.

LEAD

A nylon lead is probably the best option as it is the most resistant to puppy teeth should your pup take a liking to chewing on his lead. Of course, this is a habit that should be nipped in the bud, but if your pup likes to chew on his lead he has a very slim chance of being able to chew through the strong nylon. Nylon leads are also lightweight, which is good for a young Bichon Frise who is just getting used to the idea of walking on a lead. For everyday walking and safety purposes, the nylon lead is a good choice. As your pup grows up and gets used to walking on the lead, you may want to purchase a flexible lead. These leads allow you to extend the length to give the dog a broader area to explore or to shorten the length to keep the close to you.

COLLAR

Your pup should get used to wearing a collar all the time since you will want to attach his ID tags to it. You have to attach the lead to something! A lightweight nylon collar is a good choice; make sure that it fits snugly enough so that

Most trainers recommend using a light-weight nylon lead for your Bichon. Pet shops offer dozens of choices for collars and leads, in different styles, colours and lengths.

the pup cannot wriggle out of it, but is loose enough so that it will not be uncomfortably tight around the pup's neck. You should be able to fit a finger between the pup and the collar. It may take some time for your pup to get used to wearing the collar, but soon he will not even notice that it is there. Never use chain collars on your Bichon. Choke collars are made for training, but should only be used by an experienced handler and not on small dogs.

FOOD AND WATER BOWLS

Your pup will need two bowls, one for food and one for water. You may want two sets of bowls, one for inside and one for outside, depending on where the dog will be fed. Stainless steel or sturdy plastic bowls are popular choices. Plastic bowls are more chewable.

Dogs tend not to chew on the steel variety, which can be sterilised. It is important to buy sturdy bowls since anything is in danger of being chewed by puppy teeth and you do not want your dog to be constantly chewing apart his bowl (for his safety and for your purse!).

Provide you Bichon with feeding and watering bowls. These bowls can be constructed of sturdy plastic, ceramic, clay or stainless steel. The stainless steel ones are most dependable, durable and sanitary.

CLEANING SUPPLIES

Until a pup is housetrained you will be doing a lot of cleaning. Accidents will occur, which is okay in the beginning because the puppy does not know any better. All you can do is be prepared to clean up any 'accidents.' Old rags, towels, newspapers and a safe disinfectant are good to have on hand.

BEYOND THE BASICS

The items previously discussed are the bare necessities. You will find out what else you need as you go along—grooming supplies, flea/tick protection, baby gates to partition a room, etc. These things will vary depending on your situation but it is important that you

PHOTO COURTESY OF MIKKI PET PRODUCTS.

Choose the Right Collar

The BUCKLE COLLAR is the standard collar used for everyday purpose. Be sure that you adjust the buckle on growing puppies. Check it every day. It can become too tight overnight! These collars can be made of leather or nylon. Attach your dog's identification tags to this collar.

The CHOKE CHAIN is the usual collar recommended for training, though never for a small dog like the Bichon Frise. It is constructed of highly polished steel so that it slides easily through the stainless steel loop. The idea is that the dog controls the pressure around its neck and he will stop pulling if the collar becomes uncomfortable.

The HALTER is for a trained dog that has to be restrained to prevent running away, chasing a cat and the like. Considered the most humane of all collars, it is frequently used on smaller dogs for which collars are not comfortable.

The PRONG COLLAR certainly appears ominous, like an ancient instrument of torture. Although it is not intended to 'torture' a dog, it is only recommended on the most difficult of dogs, and *never* on a Bichon Frise or other small breeds. It should only be employed by someone who knows how to use it properly.

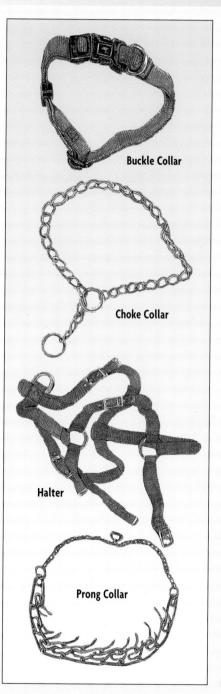

Buckle Collar

Choke Collar

Halter

Prong Collar

53

To prepare for your new puppy, you should have proper bedding, safe chew devices for teething, puppy food and a good book to show you the way.

have everything you need to feed and make your Bichon Frise comfortable in his first few days at home.

PUPPY-PROOFING YOUR HOME
Although the dog you are taking into your home will be fairly small, and therefore probably less troublesome than a larger dog, there will undoubtedly be a period of settling in. This will be great fun, but you must be prepared for mishaps around the home during the first few weeks of your life together. It will be important that precious ornaments are kept well out of harm's way, and you will have to think twice about where you place hot cups of coffee or anything breakable. Accidents can and do happen, so you will need to think ahead so as to avoid these.

Responsible law-abiding dog owners pick up their dogs' droppings whenever they are in public. Pooper-scooper devices make the job quick and easy.

Keeping your Bichon safe inside the home requires 'puppy-proofing,' which means taking precautions that your pup will not get into anything he should not

get into and that there is nothing within his reach that may harm him should he sniff it, chew it, inspect it, etc. This probably seems obvious since, whilst you

Garden Safety

Examine your lawn and garden land-scaping before bringing your puppy home. Many varieties of plants have leaves, stems or flowers that are toxic if ingested, and you can depend on a curious puppy to investigate them. Ask your veterinarian for information on poisonous plants or research them at your library.

are primarily concerned with your pup's safety, at the same time you do not want your belongings to be ruined. Breakables should be placed out of reach if your dog is to have full run of the house. If he is to be limited to certain places within the house, keep any potentially dangerous items in the 'off-limits' areas. An electrical cord can pose a danger should the puppy decide to taste it—and who is going to convince a pup that it would not make a great chew toy? Cords should be fastened tightly against the wall. If your dog is going to spend time in a crate, make sure that there is nothing near his crate that he can reach if he sticks his curious little nose or paws through the openings. Just as you would with a child, keep all household cleaners and chemicals where the pup cannot get to them.

It is also important to make sure that the outside of your home is safe. Of course your puppy should never be unsupervised, but a pup let loose in the garden will want to run and explore, and he should be granted that freedom. Do not let a fence give you a false sense of security; you would be surprised how crafty (and persistent) a dog can be in figuring out how to dig under and squeeze his way through small holes, or to jump or climb over a fence. The remedy is to make the fence high enough so that it really is impossible for your dog to get over it (about 2 metres should suffice), and well embedded into the ground. Be sure to repair or secure any gaps in the fence. Check the fence periodically to ensure that it is in good shape and make repairs as needed; a very determined pup may return to the same spot to 'work on it' until he is able to get through.

Toxic Plants

Many plants can be toxic to dogs. If you see your dog carrying a piece of vegetation in his mouth, approach him in a quiet, disinterested manner, avoid eye contact, pet him and gradually remove the plant from his mouth. Alternatively, offer him a treat and maybe he'll drop the plant on his own accord. Be sure no toxic plants are growing in your own garden.

FIRST TRIP TO THE VET

You have picked out your puppy, and your home and family are ready. Now all you have to do is collect your Bichon Frise from the breeder and the fun begins, right? Well...not so fast. Something else you need to prepare is your pup's first trip to the veterinary surgeon. Perhaps the breeder can recommend someone in the area that specialises in Bichons Frises or coated breeds, or maybe you know some other Bichon Frise owners who can suggest a good vet. Either way, you should have an appointment arranged for your pup before you pick him up and plan on taking him for an examination before bringing him home.

The pup's first visit will consist of an overall examination to make sure that the pup does not have any problems that are not apparent to the eye. The veterinary surgeon will also set up a schedule for the pup's vaccinations; the breeder will inform you of which ones the pup has already

Did You Know?

Training your puppy takes much patience and can be frustrating at times, but you should see results from your efforts. If you have a puppy that seems untrainable, take him to a trainer or behaviourist. The dog may have a personality problem that requires the help of a professional, or perhaps you need help in learning how to train your dog.

received and the vet can continue from there.

INTRODUCTION TO THE FAMILY

Everyone in the house will be excited about the puppy coming home and will want to pet him and play with him, but it is best to make the introduction low-key so as not to overwhelm the puppy. He is apprehensive already. It is the first time he has been separated from his mother and the breeder, and the ride to your home is likely the first time he has been in a car. The last thing you want to do is smother him, as this will only frighten him further. This is not to say that human contact is not extremely necessary at this stage, because this is the time when a connection between the pup and his human family is formed. Gentle petting and soothing words should help console him, as well as just putting him

Chemical Toxins

Scour your carport for potential puppy dangers. Remove weed killers, pesticides and antifreeze materials. Antifreeze is highly toxic and even a few drops can kill an adult dog. The sweet taste attracts the animal, who will quickly consume it from the floor or curbside.

down and letting him explore on his own (under your watchful eye, of course).

The pup may approach the family members or may busy himself with exploring for a while. Gradually, each person should spend some time with the pup, one at a time, crouching down to get as close to the pup's level as possible and letting him sniff their hands and petting him gently. He definitely needs human attention and he needs to be touched—this is how to form an immediate bond. Just remember that the pup is experiencing a lot of things for the first time, at the same time. There are new people, new noises, new smells, and new things to investigate: so be gentle, be affectionate, and be as comforting as you can be.

YOUR PUP'S FIRST NIGHT HOME
You have travelled home with your new charge safely in his bas-

ket or crate. He's been to the vet for a thorough check-over, he's been weighed, his papers examined; perhaps he's even been vaccinated and wormed as well. He's met the family, licked the whole family, including the excited children and the less-than-happy cat. He's explored his area, his new bed, the garden and anywhere else he's been permitted. He's eaten his first meal at home and relieved himself in the proper place. He's heard lots of new

All members of the family should handle gently the new Bichon Frise puppy as part of the socialisation process.

Puppy-Proofing

Thoroughly puppy-proof your house before bringing your puppy home. Never use roach or rodent poisons in any area accessible to the puppy. Avoid the use of toilet bowl cleaners. Most dogs are born with toilet bowl sonar and will take a drink if the lid is left open. Also keep the trash secured and out of reach.

sounds, smelled new friends and seen more of the outside world than ever before.

That was just the first day! He's worn out and is ready for bed...or so you think!

It's puppy's first night and you are ready to say 'Good night'— keep in mind that this is puppy's first night ever to be sleeping alone. His dam and littermates are no longer at paw's length and he's a bit scared, cold and lonely. Be reassuring to your new family member. This is not the time to spoil him and give in to his inevitable whining.

Puppies whine. They whine to let the others know where they are and hopefully to get company out of it. Place your pup in his new bed or crate in his room and close the door. Mercifully, he may fall asleep without a peep. If the inevitable occurs, ignore the whining: he is fine. Be strong and keep his interest in mind. Do not allow your heart to become guilty and visit the pup. He will fall asleep.

Many breeders recommend placing a piece of bedding from his former homestead in his new bed so that he recognises the scent of his littermates. Others still advise placing a hot water bottle in his bed for warmth. This latter may be a good idea provided the pup doesn't attempt to suckle— he'll get good and wet and may not fall asleep so fast.

Puppy's first night can be somewhat stressful for the pup and his new family. Remember that you are setting the tone of nighttime at your house. Unless you want to play with your pup every evening at 10 p.m., mid-night and 2 a.m., don't initiate the habit. Your family will thank you, and so will your pup!

PREVENTING PUPPY PROBLEMS
SOCIALISATION

Now that you have done all of the preparatory work and have helped your pup get accustomed to his new home and family, it is about time for you to have some fun! Socialising your Bichon Frise pup gives you the opportunity to show off your new friend, and your pup

Responsibility . . .

Grooming tools, collars, leashes, dog beds and, of course, toys will be an expense to you when you first obtain your pup, and the cost will trickle on throughout your dog's lifetime. If your puppy damages or destroys your possessions (as most puppies surely will!) or something belonging to a neighbour, you can calculate additional expense. There is also flea and pest control, which every dog owner faces more than once. You must be able to handle the financial responsibility of own-ing a dog.

How can you refuse these 'puppy-dog' eyes? Whether it's pleading for more food or the 'I-didn't-do-it' look, be consistent in enforcing the rules with your young Bichon.

gets to reap the benefits of being an adorable furry creature that people will want to pet and, in general, think is absolutely precious!

Besides getting to know his new family, your puppy should be exposed to other people, animals and situations, but of course he must not come into close contact with dogs you don't know well until his course of injections is fully complete. This will help him become well adjusted as he grows up and less prone to being timid or fearful of the new things he will encounter. Your pup's sociali-

Who's the Boss?

The majority of problems that are commonly seen in young pups will disappear as your dog gets older. However, how you deal with problems when he is young will determine how he reacts to discipline as an adult dog. It is important to establish who is boss (hopefully it will be you!) straightaway when you are first bonding wiith your dog. This bond will set the tone for the rest of your life together.

59

sation began at the breeder's but now it is your responsibility to continue it. The socialisation he receives up until the age of 12 weeks is the most critical, as this is the time when he forms his impressions of the outside world. Be especially careful during the eight-to-ten-week period, also known as the fear period. The interaction he receives during this time should be gentle and reassuring. Lack of socialisation can manifest itself in fear and aggression as the dog grows up. He

Socialisation

Thorough socialisation includes not only meeting new people but also being introduced to new experiences such as riding in the auto, having his coat brushed, hearing the television, walking in a crowd—the list is endless. The more your pup experiences, and the more positive the experiences are, the less of a shock and the less scary it will be for your pup to encounter new things.

The Bichon Frise usually is a good choice for a multiple-pet household; this is a friendly breed that gets along well with other animals.

Did You Know?

You will probably start feeding your pup the same food that he has been getting from the breeder; the breeder should give you a few days' supply to start. Although you should not give your pup too many treats, you will want to have puppy treats on hand for coaxing, training, rewards, etc. Be careful, though, as a small pup's calorie requirements are relatively low and a few treats can add up to almost a full day's worth of calories without the required nutrition.

needs lots of human contact, affection, handling and exposure to other animals.

Once your pup has received his necessary vaccinations, feel free to take him out and about (on his lead, of course). Walk him around the neighbourhood, take him on your daily errands, let people pet him, let him meet other dogs and pets, etc. Puppies do not have to try to make friends; there will be no shortage of people who will want to introduce themselves. Just make sure that you carefully supervise each meeting. If the neighbourhood

Children may want to try their hand at showing the family Bichon. Local shows are fun and a good way to get started.

children want to say hello, for example, that is great—children and pups most often make great companions. Sometimes an excited child can unintentionally handle a pup too roughly, or an overzealous pup can playfully nip a little too hard. You want to make socialisation experiences positive ones. What a pup learns during this very formative stage will impact his attitude toward future encounters. You want your dog to be comfortable around everyone. A pup that has a bad experience with a child may grow up to be a dog that is shy around or aggressive toward children.

CONSISTENCY IN TRAINING
Dogs, being pack animals, naturally need a leader, or else they try to establish dominance in their packs. When you bring a dog into your family, the choice of who becomes the leader and who becomes the 'pack' is entirely up to you! Your pup's intuitive quest for dominance, coupled with the fact that it is nearly impossible to

No Chocolate!

Use treats to bribe your dog into a desired behaviour. Try small pieces of hard cheese or freeze-dried liver. Never offer chocolate as it has toxic qualities for dogs.

look at an adorable Bichon Frise pup, with his 'puppy-dog' eyes and not cave in, give the pup almost an unfair advantage in getting the upper hand! A pup will definitely test the waters to see what he can and cannot do. Do not give in to those pleading eyes—stand your ground when it comes to disciplining the pup and make sure that all family members do the same. It will only confuse the pup when Mother tells him to get off the couch when he is used to sitting up there with Father to watch the nightly news. Avoid discrepancies by having all members of the household decide on the rules before the pup even comes home…and be consistent in enforcing them! Early training shapes the dog's personality, so you cannot be unclear in what you expect.

COMMON PUPPY PROBLEMS
The best way to prevent puppy problems is to be proactive in stopping an undesirable behaviour as soon as it starts. The old saying 'You can't teach an old dog new tricks' does not necessarily hold true, but it is true that it is much easier to discourage bad behaviour in a young developing pup than to wait until the pup's bad behaviour becomes the adult dog's bad habit. There are some problems that are especially prevalent in puppies as they develop.

NIPPING

As puppies start to teethe, they feel the need to sink their teeth into anything available...unfortunately that includes your fingers, arms, hair, and toes. You may find this behaviour cute for the first five seconds...until you feel just how sharp those puppy teeth are. This is something you want to discourage immediately and consistently with a firm 'No!' (or whatever number of firm 'No's' it takes for him to understand that you mean business). Then replace your finger with an appropriate chew toy. Whilst this behaviour is merely annoying when the dog is young, it can become dangerous as your Bichon Frise's adult teeth grow in and his jaws develop, and he continues to think it is okay to gnaw on human appendages. Your Bichon Frise does not mean any harm with a friendly nip, but he also does not know his own strength.

CRYING/WHINING

Your pup will often cry, whine, whimper, howl or make some type of commotion when he is left alone. This is basically his way of calling out for attention to make sure that you know he is there and that you have not forgotten about him. He feels insecure when he is left alone, when you are out of the house and he is in his crate or when you are in another part of the house and he cannot see you. The noise he is making is an expression of the anxiety he feels at being alone, so he needs to be taught that being alone is okay. You are not actually training the dog to stop making noise, you are training him to feel comfortable when he is alone and thus removing the need for him to make the noise. This is where the crate filled with cosy bedding and a toy comes in handy. You want to know that he is safe when you are not there to supervise, and you know that he will be safe in his crate rather than roaming freely about the house. In order for the pup to stay in his crate without making a fuss, he needs to be comfortable in his crate. On that note, it is extremely important that the crate is never used as a form of punishment, or the pup will have a negative association with the crate.

Accustom the pup to the crate in short, gradually increasing time intervals in which you put him in the crate, maybe with a treat, and stay in the room with him. If he cries or makes a fuss, do not go to him, but stay in his sight. Gradually he will realise that staying in his crate is all right without your help, and it will not be so traumatic for him when you are not around. You may want to leave the radio on softly when you leave the house; the sound of human voices may be comforting to him.

BICHON FRISE

DIETARY AND FEEDING CONSIDERATIONS

Today the choices of food for your Bichon Frise are many and varied. There are simply dozens of brands of food in all sorts of flavours and textures, ranging from puppy diets to those for seniors. There are even hypoallergenic and low-calorie diets available. Because your

Quality dog foods are more costly than generic brands but the nutritional value is well worth the added expense.

Food Preference

Selecting the best dried dog food is difficult. There is no majority consensus amongst veterinary scientists as to the value of nutrient analyses (protein, fat, fibre, moisture, ash, cholesterol, minerals, etc.). All agree that feeding trials are what matters, but you also have to consider the individual dog. Its weight, age, activity and what pleases its taste, all must be considered. It is probably best to take the advice of your veterinary surgeon. Every dog's dietary requirements vary, even during the lifetime of a particular dog.

If your dog is fed a good dried food, it does not require supplements of meat or vegetables. Dogs do appreciate a little variety in their diets so you may choose to stay with the same brand, but vary the flavour. Alternatively you may wish to add a little flavoured stock to give a difference to the taste.

Bichon Frise's food has a bearing on coat, health and temperament, it is essential that the most suitable diet is selected for a Bichon Frise of his age. It is fair to say, however, that even dedicated owners can be somewhat perplexed by the enormous range of foods available. Only understanding what is best for your dog will help you reach a valued decision.

Dog foods are produced in

though their dogs seem to like them.

When selecting your dog's diet, three stages of development must be considered: the puppy stage, adult stage and the senior or veteran stage.

PUPPY STAGE

Puppies instinctively want to suck milk from their mother's teats and a normal puppy will exhibit this behaviour from just a few moments following birth. If puppies do not attempt to suckle within the first half-hour or so, they should be encouraged to do so by placing them on a nipple, having selected ones with plenty of milk. This early milk supply is important in providing colostrum to protect the puppies during the first eight to ten weeks of their lives. Although a mother's milk is much better than any milk formula, despite there being some excellent ones available, if the puppies do not feed the breeder will have to hand-feed them. For those with

Adult and puppy Bichons Frises need different types of food and should be fed from separate bowls—this is the best way to control the type and amount of food that they are eating.

three basic types: dried, semi-moist and tinned. Dried foods are useful for the cost-conscious for overall they tend to be less expensive than semi-moist or tinned. These contain the least fat and the most preservatives. In general tinned foods are made up of 60–70 percent water, whilst semi-moist ones often contain so much sugar that they are perhaps the least preferred by owners, even

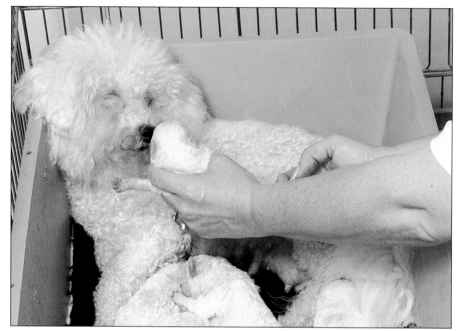

less experience, advice from a veterinary surgeon is important so that you feed not only the right quantity of milk but that of correct quality, fed at suitably frequent intervals, usually every two hours during the first few days of life.

Puppies should be allowed to nurse from their mothers for about the first six weeks, although from the third or fourth week small portions of suitable solid food can be introduced. Most breeders like to introduce alternate milk and meat meals initially, building up to weaning time.

By the time the puppies are seven or a maximum of eight weeks old, they should be fully weaned and fed solely on a proprietary puppy food. Selection of the most suitable, good-quality diet at this time is essential for a puppy's fastest growth rate is during the first year of life. Veterinary surgeons are usually able to offer advice in this regard and, although the frequency of meals will have been reduced over time, and change of diet will have been followed according to the manufacturer's instructions.

Puppy and junior diets should be well balanced for the needs of your dog, so that except in certain circumstances additional vitamins, minerals and proteins will not be required.

ADULT DIETS

A dog is considered an adult when it has stopped growing, so in general the diet of a Bichon will have been changed to an adult one by 10 or 12 months of age, sometimes sooner depending on one's selection of diet. There are many specially prepared diets available, but do keep in mind that adult Bichons seem to thrive best on a light diet with fairly low protein content. This applies particularly to those that have been spayed or castrated. It is important that you select the food best suited to your dog's needs, for active dogs will require a different diet from those leading a very sedate life.

SENIOR DIETS

As dogs get older, their metabolism changes. The older dog usually exercises less, moves more slowly and sleeps more. This change in lifestyle and physiological performance requires a change in diet. Since these changes take place slowly, they might not be recognisable. What is easily recognisable is weight gain. By continuing to feed your dog an adult-maintenance diet when it is slowing down metabolically, your dog will gain weight. Obesity in an older dog compounds the health problems that already accompany old age.

As your dog gets older, few of his organs function up to par. The

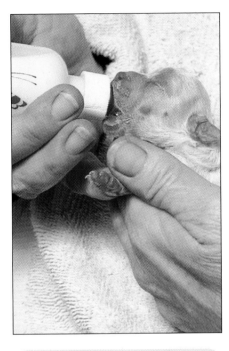

If for some reason the puppy will not suckle, or the dam will not allow it to feed, the breeder has the job of hand-feeding the puppy. The vet's advice should be sought in these situations.

Grain-Based Diets

Many adult diets are based on grain. There is nothing wrong with this as long as it does not contain soy meal. Diets based on soy often cause flatulence (passing gas).

Grain-based diets are almost always the least expensive and a good grain diet is just as good as the most expensive diet containing animal protein.

There are many cases, however, when your dog might require a special diet. These special requirements should only be recommended by your veterinary surgeon.

67

What are you feeding your dog?

Read the label on your dog food. Many dog foods only advise what 50—55% of the contents are, leaving the other 45% to doubt.

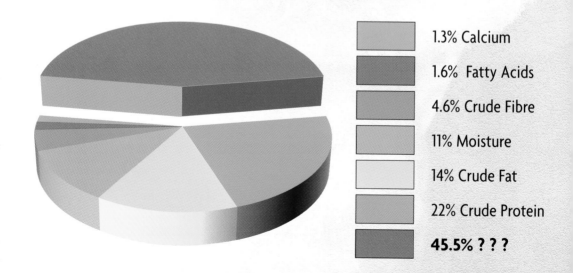

- 1.3% Calcium
- 1.6% Fatty Acids
- 4.6% Crude Fibre
- 11% Moisture
- 14% Crude Fat
- 22% Crude Protein
- **45.5% ? ? ?**

kidneys slow down and the intestines become less efficient. These age-related factors are best handled with a change in diet and a change in feeding schedule to give smaller portions that are more easily digested.

There is no single best diet for every older dog. Whilst many dogs do well on light or senior diets, other dogs do better on puppy diets or other special premium diets such as lamb and rice. Be sensitive to your senior Bichon Frise's diet and this will help control other problems that may arise with your old friend.

WATER
Just as your dog needs proper nutrition from his food, water is an essential 'nutrient' as well. Water keeps the dog's body properly hydrated and promotes normal function of the body's systems. During housebreaking it is necessary to keep an eye on how much water your Bichon Frise is drinking, but once he is reliably trained he should have access to clean fresh water at all times. Make sure that the dog's water bowl is clean, and change the water often, making sure that water is always available for your dog, especially if you feed dried food.

EXERCISE
Although a Bichon Frise is small, all dogs require some form of

exercise, regardless of breed. A sedentary lifestyle is as harmful to a dog as it is to a person. The Bichon Frise is a fairly active breed that enjoys exercise, but you don't have to be an Olympic athlete! Regular walks, play sessions in the garden, or letting the dog run free in the garden under your supervision are sufficient forms of exercise for the Bichon Frise. For those who are more ambitious, you will find that your Bichon Frise also enjoys long walks, an occasional hike or even a swim! Bear in mind that an overweight dog should never be suddenly over-exercised; instead he should be allowed to increase exercise slowly. Not only is exercise essential to keep the dog's body fit, it is essential to his men-

Don't let the Bichon's small size fool you...he needs exercise and he loves to run and play!

69

tal well being. A bored dog will find something to do, which often manifests itself in some type of destructive behaviour. In this sense, it is essential for the owner's mental well being as well!

GROOMING

Your Bichon Frise will need to be groomed regularly, so it is essential that short grooming sessions be introduced from a very early age. From the very beginning, a few minutes each day should be set aside, the duration building up slowly as the puppy matures and the coat grows in length and thickens up. Your puppy should be taught to stand on a solid surface for grooming, a suitable table on which the dog will not slip. Never, under no circumstances, leave your Bichon alone on a table, for he may all too easily jump off and harm himself.

When the puppy is used to standing on the table, you will

Your Bichon Frise must be groomed regularly. It is a process that will take some practice on the part of both you and the dog.

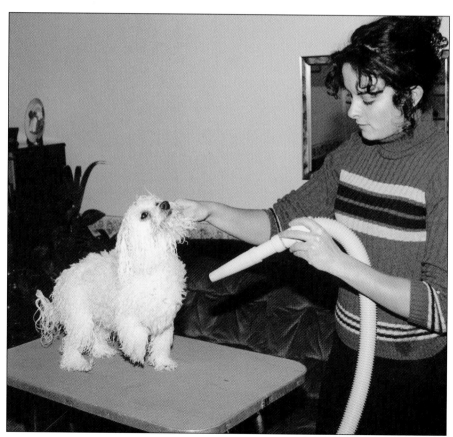

70

probably find it useful to teach him to be rolled over onto his side. This you will do by grasping his front and back legs on the opposite side of your own body, then gently placing him down by leaning over him for reassurance. To begin, just stroke his tummy so that he looks upon this new routine as something highly pleasurable. Then, when you know he is comfortable with this, introduce a few gentle brush strokes. Be sure not to hurt him at all at this stage, for this would cause him to associate this routine with discomfort. This may take a little getting used to both for you and your puppy, but if your Bichon learns to lie down on his side you will more easily be able to groom him in all the awkward places. You will both be glad you had a little patience to learn this trick from the very start!

As puppies, Bichons have only a single coat, which is soft in texture. By adulthood a double coat develops, enabling the coat to stand out from the body. This change to double coat can be a difficult time, for particular care is needed to avoid tangles being formed as the puppy coat grows out. A fully mature coat is usually significantly developing by around one year of age.

ROUTINE GROOMING
To achieve the lovely powder-puff coat for which the breed is so well

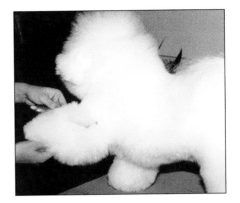

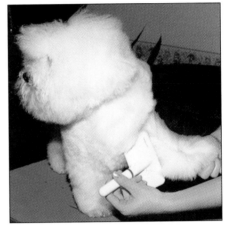

Combing, brushing and trimming are all part of the grooming process. It takes time, and perhaps professional assistance, to learn how to properly groom your Bichon Frise.

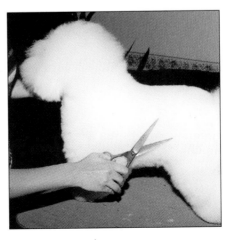

71

Trimming about the face is a necessary procedure that requires patience and a steady hand. You should start grooming your Bichon Frise puppy at an early age so that he will stand still for grooming and not make any sudden moves. The earlier you start, the more time he has to become accustomed to the grooming process.

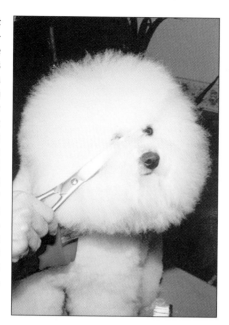

The hair on the pads of the feet should be trimmed so the dog can walk comfortably.

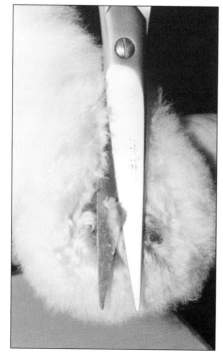

known, it is important to keep it clean and to groom regularly, even between baths. Owners who keep their Bichons as pets rather than as show dogs will still need to pay attention to the coat on a daily basis, and a trip to a professional groomer every four or five weeks is the best option. It is important not to let a Bichon's coat get out of hand, but a Bichon rescue society will always be willing to offer advice if an owner is having problems with the coat. Telephone numbers of breed rescue societies are usually available through The Kennel Club or through a Bichon breed society.

Each owner has his own favourite way of grooming his dog, and hopefully other owners with whom you come into contact will freely pass on some of their tips. Some like to begin with combing, but others feel it is necessary to use the slicker brush first of all. You will undoubtedly develop your own particular routine with the progression of time.

What is called 'line-brushing' is generally considered the most efficient method. This involves holding down one section of hair whilst gently brushing through the adjacent section using a good-quality slicker brush. Use of a poor-quality, cheap slicker brush can too easily damage the skin. It is essential to brush right through to the skin, otherwise matts will continue to form and will be left behind in the coat.

It is important to cover brushing of the entire dog in a systematic way. Most people begin with feet and legs, working over the body and lastly the head, starting above the eyes and working backward toward the skull. The tail plume on a Bichon is important and therefore this should be treated with great care in order not to remove too much hair.

Unless you are one of the owners who prefers to commence by using a comb, when brushing is completed a metal comb is used to puff up the coat, thereby creating the familiar powder-puff effect. You may choose to start at the front or the back, but be systematic. Use light strokes to lift up the coat. This is done by putting the teeth of the comb into the coat and then lifting, constantly repeating this pattern. Take care grooming the tummy and under the 'arm-pits,' for these areas are especially sensitive. Finally, gently comb through the ears and beard, and of course the tail.

Any powder used must be thoroughly brushed out of the coat prior to exhibition, and again it is a matter of personal preference whether or not powder is used. Certainly some owners find that a little powder in the coat helps avoid removing too much coat when grooming, but others use it only for cleaning stains.

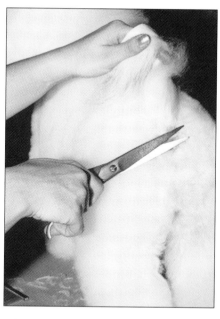

Every area of the Bichon's coat should be kept clean and neatly trimmed.

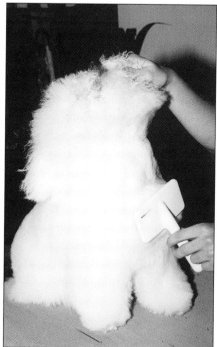

Brushing should be gentle and thorough, especially after bathing. The coat should never be left to air-dry on its own.

73

The Bichon's coat should be thoroughly wet before the shampoo is applied.

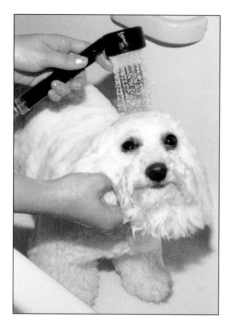

There are special shampoos for dogs, and even some specially made for white-coated dogs.

BATHING AND DRYING

How frequently you decide to bathe your Bichon Frise will depend very much on whether yours is a show dog or a pet. Show dogs are usually bathed before every show, which may be as frequently as once a week. Pet dogs are usually bathed less frequently.

As with grooming, every owner has his own preference as to how best to bathe, but ideally the coat should have been groomed through before bathing. I like to stand my own dogs on a non-slip mat in the bath, then wet the coat thoroughly using a shower. It is imperative first to test the water temperature on your own hand. Use a good-quality shampoo designed especially for dogs; indeed some are now especially suitable for the white coat of a Bichon. Always stroke the sham-

Grooming Tips

The use of human soap products like shampoo, bubble bath and hand soap can be damaging to a dog's coat and skin. Human products are too strong and remove the protective oils coating the dog's hair and skin (making him water-resistant). Use only shampoo made especially for dogs and you may like to use a medicated shampoo, which will always help to keep external parasites at bay.

poo into the coat rather than rub, so as not to create knots. When this has been thoroughly rinsed out, apply a canine conditioner in the same manner, then rinse again until the water runs clear. Many people like to use a baby shampoo on the head to avoid irritation to the eyes, and some like to plug the ears with cotton wool to avoid water getting inside them. Personally, I use neither of these, but taking care especially in that area, I have never encountered problems. Finally, lift your Bichon carefully out of the bath, wrapped in a clean towel. Undoubtedly your dog will want to shake—so be prepared!

All traces of shampoo should be thoroughly rinsed from the Bichon Frise's coat, and then the dog should be wrapped in a heavy towel and lifted from the bath.

Grooming Tips

Once you are sure that the dog is thoroughly rinsed, squeeze the excess water out of the coat with your hand and dry him with a heavy towel. You should use a blaster on his coat to encourage the coat upwards and outwards. In cold weather, never allow your dog outside with a wet coat.

There are 'dry bath' products on the market, which are sprays and powders intended for spot cleaning, that can be used between regular baths, if necessary. They are not substitutes for regular baths, but they are easy to use for touch-ups as they do not require rinsing.

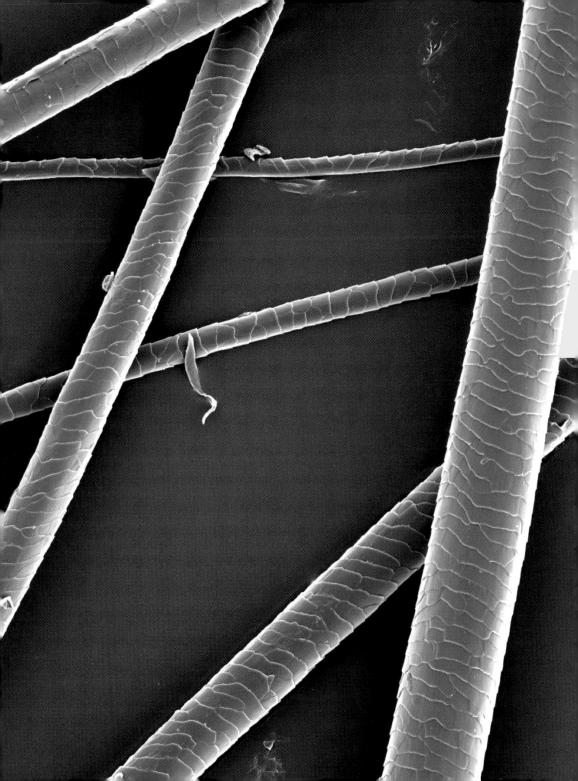

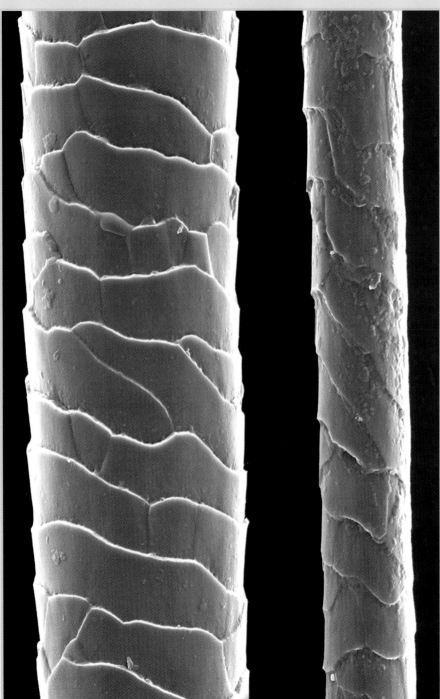

At a magnification of 750 times original size, the cuticle (outer surface) indicates the close overlapping that makes the hair so soft and resilient.

Opposite page: A magnified image of a Bichon Frise's hair magnified 200 times its original size. S.E.M. by Dr Dennis Kunkel, University of Hawaii.

77

After the dog has been thoroughly towelled, the coat should be dried fully with a blaster or hair-dryer. Be sure to aim the blast of air away from the dog's face.

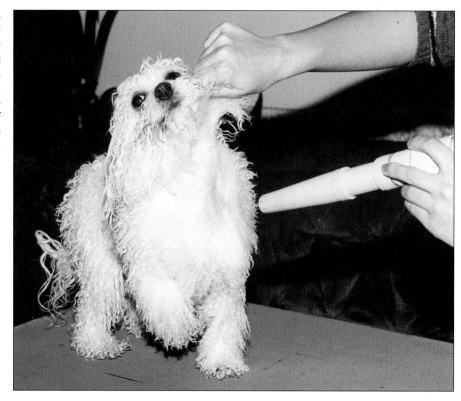

Drying can be done on whichever table you use for the grooming process. Work systematically, applying warm air from the hair-dryer. According to preference, you may use your comb or slicker brush to help separate the hair as it dries, always encouraging the coat upwards and outwards.

SCISSORING

When scissoring the coat, you will need to use long-bladed sharp scissors, so take extreme care not to injure your dog, especially when working close to the eyes.

The scissors must always be held flat on the coat when scissoring so as to achieve the desired effect.

Coat on the legs is scissored in a cylindrical fashion, not tapered in toward the foot. Also take care to hold the ears and moustache out of harm's way when scissoring the chest. Likewise, when scissoring the back end of the dog, make sure that the tail coat is moved so that it is not cut in error. Scissoring a Bichon properly is an art and takes a great deal of practice, so new Bichon owners will need to take practical guidance from others who are more experienced.

Trimming below the pads of the feet prevents uncomfortable hair-balls forming between the pads and enables the black pads of the feet to be seen. On males, most owners also trim of a little hair from the end of the penis, but a good half inch or a few centimetres must be left so that tiny hairs do not aggravate the penis and set up infection. Also, whatever you do, take care not to cut through a nipple—and remember that males have little nipples too!

EAR CLEANING

On a Bichon, hair will also grow inside the ears. This should be carefully plucked out with blunt-ended tweezers. Remove only a few hairs at a time and this should be entirely painless. Ears must always be kept clean. This can be done using specially made cotton wipes. Many people use cotton wool buds, but extreme care must be taken not to delve too deeply into the ears as this can cause injury. Be on the lookout for any signs of infection or ear mite infestation. If your Bichon Frise has been shaking his head or scratching at his ears frequently, this usually indicates a problem. If his ears have an unusual odour, this is a sure sign of mite infestation or infection, and a signal to have his ears checked by the vet.

Be especially careful when scissoring your dog's face not to endanger the dog's eyes. The scissors must be held flat on the coat in order to achieve the desired appearance.

NAIL CLIPPING

Your Bichon Frise should be accustomed to having his nails trimmed at an early age, since it will be part of your maintenance routine throughout his life. Long nails are uncomfortable for any dog and can be sharp if they scratch someone unintentionally. Also, a long nail has a better chance of ripping and bleeding, or causing the feet to spread. A good rule of thumb is that if you can hear your dog's nails clicking on the floor when he walks, his nails are too long.

Before you start cutting, make sure you can identify the 'quick' in each nail. The quick is a blood vessel that runs through the centre of each nail and grows rather

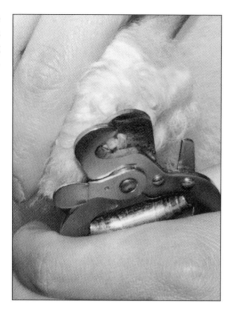

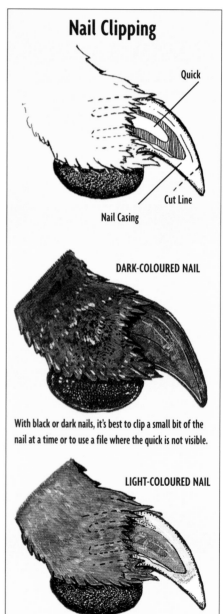

Nail Clipping

Quick

Cut Line

Nail Casing

DARK-COLOURED NAIL

With black or dark nails, it's best to clip a small bit of the nail at a time or to use a file where the quick is not visible.

LIGHT-COLOURED NAIL

In light-coloured nails, clipping is much simpler because you can see the vein (or quick) that grows inside the casing.

close to the end. It will bleed if accidentally cut, which will be quite painful for the dog as it contains nerve endings. Keep some type of clotting agent on hand, such as a styptic pencil or styptic powder (the type used for shaving). This will stop the bleeding quickly when applied to the end of the cut nail. Do not panic if this happens, just stop the bleeding and talk soothingly to your dog. Once he has calmed down, move on to the next nail. It is better to clip a little at a time, particularly with black-nailed dogs.

Hold your pup steady as you begin trimming his nails; you do not want him to make any sudden movements or run away. Talk to him soothingly and stroke him as you clip. Holding his foot in your

The area around the nose and eyes are frequently dusted with a special powder to remove the stains, as evident on this just-bathed Bichon.

hand, simply take off the end of each nail in one quick clip. You can purchase nail clippers that are specially made for dogs; you can find them wherever you buy pet or grooming supplies.

TRAVELLING WITH YOUR DOG
CAR TRAVEL

You should accustom your Bichon Frise to riding in a car at an early age. You may or may not take him in the car often, but at the very least he will need to go to the vet and you do not want these trips to be traumatic for the dog or a big hassle for you. The safest way for a dog to ride in the car is in his crate. If he uses a crate in the house, you can use the same crate for travel.

Put the pup in the crate and see how he reacts. If he seems uneasy, you can have a passenger

81

Your local pet shop will have a large supply of grooming tools that you can use on your Bichon.

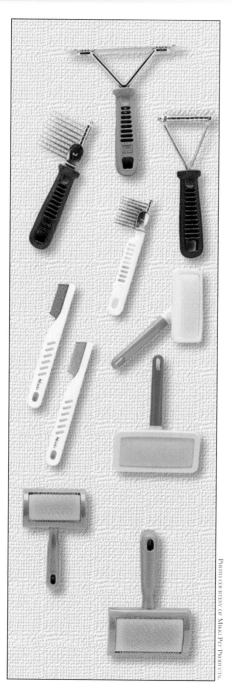

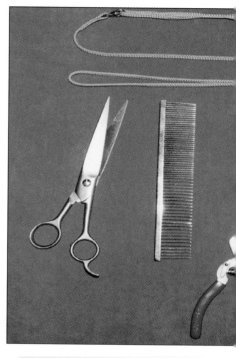

PHOTO COURTESY OF MIKKI PET PRODUCTS

Grooming Equipment

How much grooming equipment you purchase will depend on how much grooming you are going to do. Here are some basics:

- Natural bristle brush
- Slicker brush
- Metal comb
- Scissors
- Blaster
- Rubber mat
- Dog shampoo
- Spray hose attachment
- Ear cleaner
- Cotton wipes
- Towels
- Nail clippers

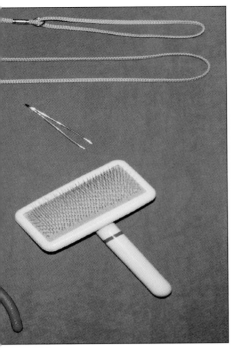

The safest method of car travel is by crate. Be sure your Bichons have proper ventilation whilst travelling.

take along some paper kitchen towels and perhaps some old towelling for use should he have an accident in the car or suffer from travel sickness.

(Center) These are the basic tools for grooming your Bichon Frise. Talk to a professional groomer to get more advice about and instruction in Bichon Frise grooming.

AIR TRAVEL

Whilst it is possible to take a dog on a flight within Britain, this is fairly unusual and advance permission is always required. The dog will be required to travel in a fibreglass crate and you should always check in advance with the airline regarding specific requirements. To help the dog be at ease, put one of his favourite toys in

hold him on his lap whilst you drive. Another option is a specially made safety harness for dogs, which straps the dog in much like a seat belt. Do not let the dog roam loose in the vehicle—this is very dangerous! If you should stop short, your dog can be thrown and injured. If the dog starts climbing on you and pestering you whilst you are driving, you will not be able to concentrate on the road. It is an unsafe situation for everyone—human and canine.

For long trips, be prepared to stop to let the dog relieve himself. Bring along whatever you need to clean up after him. You should

Travel Tip

If you are going on a long motor trip with your dog, be sure the hotels are dog friendly. Many hotels do not accept dogs. Also take along some ice that can be thawed and offered to your dog if he becomes overheated. Most dogs like to lick ice.

83

the crate with him. Do not feed the dog for at least six hours before the trip to minimise his need to relieve himself. However, certain regulations specify that water must always be made available to the dog in the crate.

Make sure your dog is properly identified and that your contact information appears on his ID tags and on his crate. Animals travel in a different area of the plane than human passengers so every rule must be strictly adhered to so as to prevent the risk of getting separated from your dog.

BOARDING
So you want to take the family holiday—and you want to include all members of the fami-

ly. You would probably make arrangements for accommodations ahead of time anyway, but this is especially important when travelling with a dog. You do not want to make an overnight stop at the only place around for miles and find out that they do not allow dogs. Also, you do not want to reserve a place for your family without confirming that you are travelling with a dog because if it is against their policy you may not have a place to stay.

Alternatively, if you are travelling and choose not to bring your Bichon Frise, you will have to make arrangements for him whilst you are away. Some options are to take him to a neighbour's house to stay

Travel Tip

For international travel you will have to make arrangements well in advance (perhaps months), as countries' regulations pertaining to bringing in animals differ. There may be special health certificates and/or vaccinations that your dog will need before taking the trip, sometimes this has to be done within a certain time frame. In rabies-free countries, you will need to bring proof of the dog's rabies vaccination and there may be a quarantine period upon arrival.

whilst you are gone, to have a trusted neighbour stop by often or stay at your house, or bring your dog to a reputable boarding kennel. If you choose to board him at a kennel, you should visit in advance to see the facility, how clean they are and where the dogs are kept. Talk to some of the employees and see how they treat the dogs—have they experience in grooming heavily coated dogs, do they spend time with the dogs, play with them, exercise them, etc.? Also find out the kennel's policy on vaccinations and what they require. This is for all of the dogs' safety, since when dogs are kept together, there is a greater risk of diseases being passed from dog to dog.

IDENTIFICATION

Your Bichon Frise is your valued companion and friend. That is why you always keep a close eye on him and you have made sure that he cannot escape from the garden or wriggle out of his collar and run away from you. However, accidents can happen and there may come a time when your dog unexpectedly gets separated from you. If this unfortunate event should occur, the first thing on your mind will be finding him. Proper identification, including an ID tag, a tattoo and possibly a microchip, will increase the chances of his being returned to you safely and quickly.

Identification

If your dog gets lost, he is not able to ask for directions home.

Identification tags fastened to the collar give important information—the dog's name, the owner's name, the owner's address and a telephone number where the owner can be reached. This makes it easy for whoever finds the dog to contact the owner and arrange to have the dog returned. An added advantage is that a person will be more likely to approach a lost dog who has ID tags on his collar; it tells the person that this is somebody's pet rather than a stray. This is the easiest and fastest method of identification provided that the tags stay on the collar and the collar stays on the dog.

You may find it necessary to board your dog on occasion. Your veterinary surgeon can help you select a proper kennel, or you can visit the local kennels to find one with clean quarters, ample room for your dog and a knowledgeable caring staff that has experience with coated breeds.

85

Housebreaking and Training Your
BICHON FRISE

Living with an untrained dog is a lot like owning a piano that you do not know how to play—it is a nice object to look at but it does not do much more than that to bring you pleasure. Now try taking piano lessons and suddenly the piano comes alive and brings forth magical sounds and rhythms that set your heart singing and your body swaying.

The same is true with your Bichon. Any dog is a big responsibility and if not trained sensibly may develop unacceptable behaviour that annoys you or could even cause

family friction.

To train your Bichon, you may like to enrol in an obedience class. Teach him good manners as

Did You Know?

Taking your dog to an obedience school may be the best investment in time and money you can ever make. You will enjoy the benefits for the lifetime of your dog and you will have the opportunity to meet people with your similar expectations for companion dogs.

you learn how and why he behaves the way he does. Find out how to communicate with your dog and how to recognise and understand his communications with you. Suddenly the dog takes on a new role in your life—he is smart, interesting, well behaved and fun to be with. He demonstrates his bond of devotion to you daily. In other words, your Bichon does wonders for your ego because he constantly reminds you that you are not only his leader, you are his hero!

Those involved with teaching dog obedience and counselling owners about their dogs' behav-

Patience . . .

If you start with a normal, healthy dog and give him time, patience and some carefully executed lessons, you will reap the rewards of that training for the life of the dog. And what a life it will be! The two of you will find immeasurable pleasure in the companionship you have built together with love, respect and understanding. Good luck and enjoy!

It is up to you to select the 'toilet area' for your Bichon, else he may end up relieving himself in areas you'd rather he wouldn't.

iour have discovered some interesting facts about dog ownership. For example, training dogs when they are puppies results in the highest rate of success in developing well-mannered and well-adjusted adult dogs. Training an older dog, from six months to six years of age, can produce almost equal results providing that the owner accepts the dog's slower rate of learning capability and is willing to work patiently to help the dog succeed at developing to his fullest potential. Unfortunately, many owners of untrained adult dogs lack the patience factor, so they do not persist until their dogs are successful at learning particular behaviours.

Training a puppy aged 10 to 16 weeks (20 weeks at the most) is like working with a dry sponge in a pool of water. The pup soaks up whatever you show him and constantly looks for more things to do and learn. At this early age, his

Did You Know?

Training a dog is a life experience. Many parents admit that much of what they know about raising children they learned from caring for their dogs. Dogs respond to love, fairness and guidance, just as children do. Become a good dog owner and you may become an even better parent.

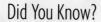

body is not yet producing hormones, and therein lies the reason for such a high rate of success. Without hormones, he is focused on his owners and not particularly interested in investigating other

places, dogs, people, etc. You are his leader: his provider of food, water, shelter and security. He latches onto you and wants to stay close. He will usually follow you from room to room, will not let you out of his sight when you are outdoors with him, and will respond in like manner to the people and animals you

encounter. If you greet a friend warmly, he will be happy to greet the person as well. If, however, you are hesitant, even anxious, about the approach of a stranger, he will respond accordingly.

Once the puppy begins to produce hormones, his natural curiosity emerges and he begins to investigate the world around him. It is at this time when you may notice that the untrained dog begins to wander away from you and even ignore your commands to stay close. When this behaviour becomes a problem, the owner has two choices: get rid of the dog or train him. It is strongly urged that you choose the latter option.

There are usually classes within a reasonable distance from the owner's home, but you also do a lot to train your dog yourself. Sometimes there are classes available but the tuition is too costly. Whatever the circumstances, the solution to the problem of lack of lesson availability lies within the

Training Tip

Dogs are sensitive to their master's moods and emotions. Use your voice wisely when communicating with your dog. Never raise your voice at your dog unless you are angry and trying to correct him. 'Barking' at your dog can become as meaningless as 'dogspeak' is to you. Think before you bark!

Becoming toilet trained is the minimum you should expect from your dog; he also must learn basic commands such as Sit, Heel, Come and Stay. Do not settle for anything less, even if you have to engage a professional trainer to help you.

You should 'train' yourself to clean up any canine deposits produced by your dog regardless of where they occur—inside or outside your garden.

pages of this book.

This chapter is devoted to helping you train your Bichon at home. If the recommended procedures are followed faithfully, you may expect positive results that will prove rewarding to both you and your dog.

Whether your new charge is a puppy or a mature adult, the methods of teaching and the techniques we use in training basic behaviours are the same. After all, no dog, whether puppy or adult, likes harsh or inhumane methods. All creatures, however, respond favourably to gentle motivational methods and sincere praise and encouragement. Now let us get started.

Getting Your Attention

Dogs will do anything for your attention. If you reward the dog when he is calm and resting, you will develop a well-mannered dog. If, on the other hand, you greet your dog excitedly and encourage him to wrestle and roughhouse with you, the dog will greet you the same way and you will have a hyper dog on your hands.

Training Tip

Dogs are the most honourable animals in existence. They consider another species (humans) as their own. They interface with you. You are their leader. Puppies perceive children to be on their level: their actions around small children are different than their behaviour around their adult masters

HOUSEBREAKING

You can train a puppy to relieve itself wherever you choose, but this must be somewhere suitable. You should bear in mind from the outset that when your puppy is old enough to go out in public places, any canine deposits must be removed at once. You will always have to carry with you a small plastic bag or 'poop-scoop.'

Outdoor training includes such surfaces as grass, dirt and cement. Indoor training usually means training your dog to newspaper.

When deciding on the surface

Training Tip

Your dog is actually training you at the same time you are training him. Dogs do things to get attention. They usually repeat whatever succeeds in getting your attention.

Canine Development Schedule

It is important to understand how and at what age a puppy develops into adulthood. If you are a puppy owner, consult the following Canine Development Schedule to determine the stage of development your puppy is currently experiencing. This knowledge will help you as you work with the puppy in the weeks and months ahead.

Period	Age	Characteristics
First to Third	**Birth to Seven Weeks**	Puppy needs food, sleep and warmth, and responds to simple and gentle touching. Needs mother for security and disciplining. Needs littermates for learning and interacting with other dogs. Pup learns to function within a pack and learns pack order of dominance. Begin socialising with adults and children for short periods. Begins to become aware of its environment.
Fourth	**Eight to Twelve Weeks**	Brain is fully developed. Needs socialising with outside world. Remove from mother and littermates. Needs to change from canine pack to human pack. Human dominance necessary. Fear period occurs between 8 and 16 weeks. Avoid fright and pain.
Fifth	**Thirteen to Sixteen Weeks**	Training and formal obedience should begin. Less association with other dogs, more with people, places, situations. Period will pass easily if you remember this is pup's change-to-adolescence time. Be firm and fair. Flight instinct prominent. Permissiveness and over-disciplining can do permanent damage. Praise for good behaviour.
Juvenile	**Four to Eight Months**	Another fear period about 7 to 8 months of age. It passes quickly, but be cautious of fright and pain. Sexual maturity reached. Dominant traits established. Dog should understand sit, down, come and stay by now.

NOTE: THESE ARE APPROXIMATE TIME FRAMES. ALLOW FOR INDIVIDUAL DIFFERENCES IN PUPPIES.

and location that you will want your Bichon to use, be sure it is going to be permanent. Training your dog to grass and then changing your mind two months later is extremely difficult for both dog and owner.

Next, choose the command you will use each and every time you want your puppy to void. 'Go hurry up' and 'Toilet' are examples of commands commonly used by dog owners.

Get in the habit of giving the puppy your chosen relief command before you take him out.

Training Tip

Do not carry your dog to his toilet area. Lead him there on a leash or, better yet, encourage him to fol-

low you to the spot. If you start carrying him to his spot, you might end up doing this routine forever and your dog will have the satisfaction of having trained YOU.

Training Tip

Stand up straight and authoritatively when giving your dog commands. Do not issue commands when lying on the floor or lying on your back on the sofa. If you are on your hands and knees when you give a command, your dog will think you are positioning yourself to play.

That way, when he becomes an adult, you will be able to determine if he wants to go out when you ask him. A confirmation will be signs of interest, wagging his tail, watching you intently, going to the door, etc.

PUPPY'S NEEDS
Puppy needs to relieve himself after play periods, after each meal, after he has been sleeping and any time he indicates that he is looking for a place to urinate or defecate.

The urinary and intestinal tract muscles of very young puppies are not fully developed. Therefore, like human babies, puppies need to relieve themselves frequently.

Take your puppy out often—every hour for an eight-week-old, for example, and always immediately after sleeping and eating. The older the puppy, the less often he will need to relieve him-

How Many Times a Day?

AGE	RELIEF TRIPS
To 14 weeks	10
14–22 weeks	8
22–32 weeks	6
Adulthood	4
(dog stops growing)	

These are estimates, of course, but they are a guide to the MINIMUM opportunities a dog should have each day to relieve itself.

A look that can melt a heart of steel! Puppies must relieve themselves on a regular basis, especially after meals, play periods and sleeping. This early training is very important. You want him to relieve himself in an area with which both of you are comfortable.

self. Finally, as a mature healthy adult, he will require only three to five relief trips per day.

HOUSING

Since the types of housing and control you provide for your puppy has a direct relationship on the success of housetraining, we consider the various aspects of both before we begin training.

Bringing a new puppy home and turning him loose in your house can be compared to turning a child loose in a sports arena and telling the child that the place is all his! The sheer enormity of the place would be too much for him to handle.

Instead, offer the puppy clearly defined areas where he can play, sleep, eat and live. A room of the house where the family gathers is the most obvious choice. Puppies are social animals

and need to feel a part of the pack right from the start. Hearing your voice, watching you whilst you are doing things and smelling you nearby are all positive reinforcers

Housebreaking Tip

Never line your pup's sleeping area with newspaper. Bichon pups should not be kept on newspaper with print as it mars their white coats. Puppy litters are usually raised on newspaper and, once in your home, the puppy will immediately associate newspaper with voiding. Never put newspaper on any floor while housetraining, as this will only confuse the puppy. If you are paper-training him, use paper in his designated relief area ONLY. Finally, restrict water intake after evening meals. Offer a few licks at a time—never let a young puppy gulp water after meals.

93

that he is now a member of your pack. Usually a family room, the kitchen or a nearby adjoining breakfast area is ideal for providing safety and security for both puppy and owner.

Within that room there should be a smaller area which the puppy can call his own. An alcove, a wire or fibreglass dog crate or a fenced (not boarded!) corner from which he can view the activities of his new family will be fine. The size of the area or crate is the key factor here. The area must be large enough

The Golden Rule

The golden rule of dog training is simple. For each 'question' (command), there is only one correct answer (reaction). One command = one reaction. Keep practising the command until the dog reacts correctly without hesitating. Be repetitive but not monotonous. Dogs get bored just as people do!

top, yet small enough so that he cannot relieve himself at one end and sleep at the other without coming into contact with his droppings until fully trained to relieve himself outside.

Dogs are, by nature, clean animals and will not remain close to their relief areas unless forced to do so. In those cases, they then become dirty dogs and usually remain that way for life.

The designated area should be lined with clean bedding and a toy. Water must always be available, in a non-spill container.

Exercise

The puppy should also have regular play and exercise sessions when he is with you or a family member. Exercise for a very young puppy can consist of a short walk around the house or garden. Playing can include fetching games with a large ball or a special raggy. (All puppies teethe and need soft things upon which to chew.) Remember to restrict play periods to indoors within his living area (the family room for example) until he is completely housetrained.

for the puppy to lie down and stretch out as well as stand up without rubbing his head on the

CONTROL

By control, we mean helping the puppy to create a lifestyle pattern that will be compatible to that of his human pack (YOU!). Just as we guide little children to learn our way of life, we must show the puppy when it is time to play, eat, sleep, exercise and even entertain himself.

Your puppy should always

You must determine how you want your Bichon Frise to behave. If you allow your dogs on the furniture, you may want to protect it with a cover or easily cleaned blanket.

sleep in his crate. He should also learn that, during times of household confusion and excessive human activity such as at breakfast when family members are preparing for the day, he can play by himself in relative safety and comfort in his designated area. Each time you leave the puppy alone, he should understand exactly where he is to stay. Puppies are chewers. They cannot tell the difference between lamp cords, television wires, shoes, table legs, etc. Chewing into a television wire, for example, can be fatal to the puppy whilst a shorted wire can start a fire in the house.

If the puppy chews on the arm of the chair when he is alone, you will probably discipline him

Training Tip

Dogs are as different from each other as people are. What works for one dog may not work for another. Have an open mind. If one method of training is unsuccessful, try another.

95

Bichon Frise

angrily when you get home. Thus, he makes the association that your coming home means he is going to be punished. (He will not remember chewing up the chair and is incapable of making the association of the discipline with his naughty deed.)

Other times of excitement, such as family parties, etc., can be fun for the puppy providing he can view the activities from the security of his designated area. He is not underfoot and he is not being fed all sorts of titbits that will

THE SUCCESS METHOD
6 Steps to Successful Crate Training

1 Tell the puppy 'Crate time!' and place him in the crate with a small treat (a piece of cheese or half of a biscuit). Let him stay in the crate for five minutes while you are in the same room. Then release him and praise lavishly. Never release him when he is fussing. Wait until he is quiet before you let him out.

2 Repeat Step 1 several times a day.

3 The next day, place the puppy in the crate as before. Let him stay there for ten minutes. Do this several times.

4 Continue building time in five-minute increments until the puppy

stays in his crate for 30 minutes with you in the room. Always take him to his relief area after prolonged periods in his crate.

5 Now go back to Step 1 and let the puppy stay in his crate for five minutes, this time while you are out of the room.

6 Once again, build crate time in five-minute increments with you out of the room. When the puppy will stay willingly in his crate (he may even fall asleep!) for 30 minutes with you out of the room, he will be ready to stay in it for several hours at a time.

probably cause him stomach distress, yet he still feels a part of the fun.

SCHEDULE

A puppy should be taken to his relief area each time he is released from his designated area, after meals, after a play session, when he first awakens in the morning (at age eight weeks, this can mean 5 a.m.!). The puppy will indicate that he's ready 'to go' by circling or sniffing busily—-do not misinterpret these signs. For a puppy less than ten weeks of age, a routine of taking him out every hour is necessary. As the puppy grows, he will be able to wait for longer periods of time.

Keep trips to his relief area short. Stay no more than five or six minutes and then return to the house. If he goes during that time, praise him lavishly and take him indoors immediately. If he does not, but he has an accident when

Rules to Obey

If you want to be successful in training your dog, you have four rules to obey yourself:
1. Develop an understanding of how a dog thinks.
2. Do not blame the dog for lack of communication.
3. Define your dog's personality and act accordingly.
4. Have patience and be consistent.

Be Consistent

Most of all, be consistent. Always take your dog to the same location, always use the same command, and always have him on lead when he is in his relief area, unless a fenced-in garden is available.

By following the Success Method, your puppy will be completely housetrained by the time his muscle and brain development reach maturity. Keep in mind that small breeds usually mature faster than large breeds, but all puppies should be trained by six months of age.

you go back indoors, pick him up immediately, say 'No! No!' and return to his relief area. Wait a few minutes, then return to the house again. never hit a puppy or rub his face in urine or excrement when he has an accident!

Once indoors, put the puppy in his crate until you have had time to clean up his accident. Then release him to the family area and watch him more closely than before. Chances are, his accident was a result of your not picking up his signal or waiting too long before offering him the opportunity to relieve himself. Never hold a grudge against the puppy for accidents.

A wire crate offers your Bichon many advantages. In warmer climes, the wire crate is ideal for ventilation. Most Bichons like to be able to see what's going on about them.

Let the puppy learn that going outdoors means it is time to relieve himself, not play. Once trained, he will be able to play indoors and out and still differentiate between the times for play versus the times for relief.

Help him develop regular hours for naps, being alone, playing by himself and just resting, all in his crate. Encourage him to entertain himself whilst you are busy with your activities. Let him learn that having you near is comforting, but it is not your main purpose in life to provide him with undivided attention.

Each time you put a puppy in his own area, use the same command, whatever suits best. Soon, he will run to his crate or special area when he hears you say those words.

Crate training provides safety for you, the puppy and the home. It also provides the puppy with a feeling of security, and that helps the puppy achieve self-confidence and clean habits.

Remember that one of the primary ingredients in housetraining your puppy is control. Regardless of your lifestyle, there will always be occasions when you will need to have a place where your dog can stay and be happy and safe. Training is the answer for now and in the future.

In conclusion, a few key elements are really all you need for a successful house training method—consistency, frequency, praise, control and supervision. By following these procedures with a normal, healthy puppy, you and the puppy will soon be past the stage of 'accidents' and ready to move on to a full and rewarding life together.

ROLES OF DISCIPLINE, REWARD AND PUNISHMENT

Discipline, training one to act in accordance with rules, brings

Be Consistent

By providing sleeping and resting quarters that fit the dog, and offering frequent opportunities to relieve himself outside his quarters, the puppy quickly learns that the outdoors (or the newspaper if you are training him to paper) is the place to go when he needs to urinate or defecate. It also reinforces his innate desire to keep his sleeping quarters clean. This, in turn, helps develop the muscle control that will eventually produce a dog with clean living habits.

order to life. It is as simple as that. Without discipline, particularly in a group society, chaos reigns supreme and the group will eventually perish. Humans and canines are social animals and need some form of discipline in order to function effectively. They must procure food, protect their home base and their young and reproduce to keep the species going.

If there were no discipline in the lives of social animals, they would eventually die from starvation and/or predation by other stronger animals.

In the case of domestic canines, dogs need discipline in their lives in order to understand how their pack (you and other family members) functions and how they must act in order to survive.

A large humane society in a highly populated area recently surveyed dog owners regarding their satisfaction with their relationships with their dogs. People who had trained their dogs were 75% more satisfied with their pets than those who had never trained their dogs.

Dr. Edward Thorndike, a psychologist, established *Thorndike's Theory of Learning*, which states that a behaviour that results in a pleasant event tends to be repeated. A behaviour that results in an unpleasant event tends not to be repeated. It is this theory on which training methods are based today. For example, if you manipulate a dog to perform a specific behaviour and reward him for doing it, he is likely to do it again because he enjoyed the end result.

Occasionally, punishment, a penalty inflicted for an offence, is necessary. The best type of punishment often comes from an outside source. For example, a child is told not to touch the stove because he may get burned. He disobeys and touches the stove. In doing so, he receives a burn. From that time on, he respects the heat of the stove and avoids contact with it. Therefore, a behaviour that results in an unpleasant event tends not to be repeated.

Practice Makes Perfect

• Have training lessons with your dog every day in several short segments—three to five times a day for a few minutes at a time is ideal.

• Do not have long practice sessions. The dog will become easily bored.

• Never practice when you are tired, ill, worried or in an otherwise negative mood. This will transmit to the dog and may have an adverse effect on its performance.

Think fun, short and above all POSITIVE! End each session on a high note, rather than a failed exercise, and make sure to give a lot of praise. Enjoy the training and help your dog enjoy it, too.

A good example of a dog learning the hard way is the dog who chases the house cat. He is told many times to leave the cat alone, yet he persists in teasing the cat. Then, one day he begins chasing the cat but the cat turns and swipes a claw across the dog's face, leaving him with a painful gash on his nose. The final result is that the dog stops chasing the cat.

TRAINING EQUIPMENT
COLLAR AND LEAD
For a Bichon the collar and lead that you use for training must be one with which you are easily able to work, not too heavy for the dog and perfectly safe.

Training Tip
Dogs do not understand our language. They can be trained to react to a certain sound, at a certain volume. If you say 'No, Oliver' in a very soft pleasant voice it will not have the same meaning as 'No, Oliver!!' when you shout it as loud as you can. You should never use the dog's name during a reprimand, just the command NO!! Since dogs don't understand words, comics use dogs trained with opposite meanings. Thus, when the comic commands his dog to SIT the dog will stand up; and vice versa.

Training Tip
If you have other pets in the home and/or interact often with the pets of friends and other family members, your pup will respond to those pets in much the same manner as you do. It is only when you show fear or resentment toward another animal that he will act fearful or unfriendly.

TREATS
Have a bag of treats on hand. Something nutritious and easy to swallow works best. Use a soft treat, a chunk of cheese or a piece of cooked chicken rather than a dry biscuit. By the time the dog gets done chewing a dry treat, he will forget why he is being rewarded in the first place! Using food rewards will not teach a dog to beg at the table—the only way to teach a dog to beg at the table is to give him food from the table. In training, rewarding the dog with a food treat will help him associate praise and the treats with learning new behaviours that obviously please his owner.

TRAINING BEGINS:
ASK THE DOG A QUESTION
In order to teach your dog anything, you must first get his attention. After all, he cannot learn anything if he is looking away from you with his mind on something else.

Did You Know?

Play fetch games with your puppy in an enclosed area where he can

retrieve his toy and bring it back to you. Always use a toy or object designated just for this purpose. Never use a shoe, sock or other item he may later confuse with those in your closet or underneath your chair.

To get his attention, ask him, 'School?' and immediately walk over to him and give him a treat as you tell him 'Good dog.' Wait a minute or two and repeat the routine, this time with a treat in your hand as you approach within a foot of the dog. Do not go directly to him, but stop about a foot short of him and hold out the treat as you ask, 'School?' He will see you approaching with a treat in your hand and most likely begin walking toward you. As you meet, give

him the treat and praise again.

The third time, ask the question, have a treat in your hand and walk only a short distance toward the dog so that he must walk almost all the way to you. As he reaches you, give him the treat and praise again.

By this time, the dog will probably be getting the idea that if he pays attention to you, especially when you ask that question, it will pay off in treats and fun activities for him. In other words, he learns that 'school' means doing fun things with you that result in treats and positive attention for him.

Remember that the dog does not understand your verbal language, he only recognises sounds. Your question translates to a series of sounds for him, and those sounds become the signal to go to you and pay attention; if he does, he will get to interact with you plus receive treats and praise.

Training Tip

Never train your dog, puppy or adult, when you are mad or in a sour mood. Dogs are very sensitive to human feelings, especially anger, and if your dog senses that you are angry or upset, he will connect your anger with his training and learn to resent or fear his training sessions.

from their owners and feel so proud of themselves whenever they accomplish a behaviour.

You will not use food forever in getting the dog to obey your commands. Food is only used to teach new behaviours, and once the dog knows what you want when you give a specific command, you will wean him off of the food treats but still maintain the verbal praise. After all, you will always have your voice with you, and there will be many times when you have no food rewards but expect the dog to obey.

TEACHING DOWN
Teaching the down exercise is easy when you understand how the dog perceives the down position, and it is very difficult when you do not. Dogs perceive the down position as a submissive one, therefore teaching the down exercise using a forceful method can sometimes make the dog develop such a fear of the down that he either runs away when you say 'Down' or he attempts to snap at the person who tries to force him down.

Have the dog sit close alongside your left leg, facing in the same direction as you are. Hold the lead in your left hand and a food treat in your right. Now place your left hand lightly on the top of the dog's shoulders where they meet above the spinal cord. Do not push down on the dog's

Do not try to teach the down exercise by forcing your dog into the down position. Instead, guide him gently while reassuring him and perhaps coaxing with a treat.

THE BASIC COMMANDS
TEACHING SIT
Now that you have the dog's attention, attach his lead and hold it in your left hand and a food treat in your right. Place your food hand at the dog's nose and let him lick the treat but not take it from you. Say 'Sit' and slowly raise your food hand from in front of the dog's nose up over his head so that he is looking at the ceiling. As he bends his head upward, he will have to bend his knees to maintain his balance. As he bends his knees, he will assume a sit position. At that point, release the food treat and praise lavishly with comments such as 'Good dog! Good sit!', etc. Remember to always praise enthusiastically, because dogs relish verbal praise

Training Tip

A dog in jeopardy never lies down. He stays alert on his feet because instinct tells him that he may have to run away or fight for his survival. Therefore, if a dog feels threatened or anxious, he will not lie down. Consequently, it is important to have the dog calm and relaxed as he learns the down exercise.

shoulders; simply rest your left hand there so you can guide the dog to lie down close to your left leg rather than to swing away from your side when he drops.

Now place the food hand at the dog's nose, say 'Down' very softly (almost a whisper), and slowly lower the food hand to the dog's front feet. When the food hand reaches the floor, begin moving it forward along the floor in front of the dog. Keep talking softly to the dog, saying things like, 'Do you want this treat? You can do this, good dog.' Your reassuring tone of voice will help calm the dog as he tries to follow the food hand in order to get the treat.

When the dog's elbows touch the floor, release the food and praise softly. Try to get the dog to maintain that down position for several seconds before you let him sit up again. The goal here is to get the dog to settle down and not feel threatened.

Use your voice and hand signals to train your Bichon Frise to sit and stay. Have patience and be sure to make eye contact when training your dog.

103

soon as you get back to the original position, release the food and praise lavishly.

To teach the down/stay, do the down as previously described. As soon as the dog lies down, say 'Stay' and step out on your right foot just as you did in the sit/stay. Count to five and then return to stand beside the dog with him on your left side. Release the treat and praise as always.

Within a week or ten days, you can begin to add a bit of distance between you and your dog when you leave him. When you do, use your left hand open with the palm facing the dog as a stay signal, much the same as the hand signal a police officer uses to stop traffic at an intersection. Hold the food treat in your right hand as before, but this time the food is not touching the dog's nose. He will watch the food hand and quickly learn that he is going to get that treat as soon as you return to his side.

When you can stand 1 metre away from your dog for 30 seconds, you can then begin building time and distance in both stays. Eventually, the dog can be expected to remain in the stay position for prolonged periods of time until you return to him or call him to you. Always praise lavishly when he stays.

A food reward or a favourite toy are two good motivators to ensure that the dog will happily come to you.

TEACHING STAY

It is easy to teach the dog to stay in either a sit or a down position. Again, we use food and praise during the teaching process as we help the dog to understand exactly what it is that we are expecting him to do.

To teach the sit/stay, start with the dog sitting on your left side as before and hold the lead in your left hand. Have a food treat in your right hand and place your food hand at the dog's nose. Say 'Stay' and step out on your right foot to stand directly in front of the dog, toe to toe, as he licks and nibbles the treat. Be sure to keep his head facing upward to maintain the sit position. Count to five and then swing around to stand next to the dog again with him on your left. As

TEACHING COME

If you make teaching 'come' a fun experience, you should never have a 'student' that does not love the game or that fails to come when called. The secret, it seems, is never to teach the word 'come.'

At times when an owner most wants his dog to come when called, the owner is likely upset or anxious and he allows these feelings to come through in the tone of his voice when he calls his dog. Hearing that desperation in his owner's voice, the dog fears the results of going to him and therefore either disobeys outright or runs in the opposite direction. The secret, therefore, is to teach the dog a game and, when you want him to come to you, simply play the game. It is practically a no-fail solution!

To begin, have several members of your family take a few food treats and each go into a different room in the house. Take turns calling the dog, and each person should celebrate the dog's

Training Tip

Never call your dog to come to you for a correction or scold him when he reaches you. That is the quickest way to turn a 'Come' command into 'Go away fast!' Dogs think only in the present tense and he will connect the scolding with coming to his master, not with the misbehaviour of a few moments earlier.

Success Method

Success that comes by luck is usually short lived. Success that comes by well-thought-out proven methods is often more easily achieved and permanent. This is the Success Method. It is designed to give you, the puppy owner, a simple yet proven way to help your puppy develop clean living habits and a feeling of security in his new environment.

finding him with a treat and lots of happy praise. When a person calls the dog, he is actually inviting the dog to find him and get a treat as a reward for 'winning.'

A few turns of the 'Where are you?' game and the dog will figure out that everyone is playing the game and that each person has a big celebration awaiting his success at locating them. Once he learns to love the game, simply calling out 'Where are you?' will bring him running from wherever he is when he hears that all-important question.

The come command is recognised as one of the most important things to teach a dog, but there are trainers who work with thousands of dogs and never teach the actual word 'Come.' Yet these dogs will race to respond to a person who uses the dog's name followed by 'Where are you?' For example, a woman has a 12-year-old companion dog who went

Training Tip

When calling the dog, do not say 'Come.' Say things like, 'Rover, where are you? See if you can find me! I have a cookie for you!' Keep up a constant line of chatter with coaxing sounds and frequent questions such as, 'Where are you?' The dog will learn to follow the sound of your voice to locate you and receive his reward.

Training your dog to heel means the dog should follow you closely regardless of the speed of your movements. He should keep pace beside you when you are running as well as walking.

blind, but who never fails to locate her owner when asked, 'Where are you?'

Children particularly love to play this game with their dogs. Children can hide in smaller places like a shower or bathtub, behind a bed or under a table. The dog needs to work a little bit harder to find these hiding places, but when he does he loves to celebrate with a treat and a tussle with a favourite youngster.

TEACHING HEEL

Heeling means that the dog walks beside the owner without pulling. It takes time and patience on the owner's part to succeed at teaching the dog that he (the owner) will not proceed unless the dog is walking calmly beside him. Pulling out ahead on the lead is definitely not acceptable.

Begin with holding the lead in your left hand as the dog sits beside your left leg. Move the loop end of the lead to your right hand but keep your left hand short on the lead so it keeps the dog in close next to you.

Say 'Heel' and step forward on your left foot. Keep the dog close to you and take three steps. Stop and have the dog sit next to you in what we now call the 'heel position.' Praise verbally, but do

Training Tip

Teach your dog to HEEL in an enclosed area. Once you think the dog will obey reliably and you want to attempt advanced obedience exercises such as off-lead heeling, test him in a fenced in area so he cannot run away.

not touch the dog. Hesitate a moment and begin again with 'Heel,' taking three steps and stopping, at which point the dog is told to sit again.

Your goal here is to have the dog walk those three steps without pulling on the lead. When he will walk calmly beside you for three steps without pulling, increase the number of steps you take to five. When he will walk politely beside you whilst you take five steps, you can increase the length of your walk to ten steps. Keep increasing the length of your stroll until the dog will walk quietly beside you without pulling as long as you want him to heel. When you stop heeling, indicate to the dog that the exercise is over by verbally praising as you pet him and say 'OK, good dog.' The 'OK' is used as a release word meaning that the exercise is finished and the dog is free to relax.

If you are dealing with a dog who insists on pulling you

Training Tip

If you begin teaching the heel by taking long walks and letting the dog pull you along, he misinterprets this action as an acceptable form of taking a walk. When you pull back on the lead to counteract his pulling, he reads that tug as a signal to pull even harder!

Heeling means that the dog should walk alongside you exactly as shown in this photograph. The dog should neither be pulling on the lead ahead of you nor lagging behind.

107

around, simply 'put on your brakes' and stand your ground until the dog realises that the two of you are not going anywhere until he is beside you and moving at your pace, not his. It may take some time just standing there to convince the dog that you are the leader and you will be the one to decide on the direction and speed of your travel.

Each time the dog looks up at you or slows down to give a slack lead between the two of you, quietly praise him and say, 'Good heel. Good dog.' Eventually, the dog will begin to respond and within a few days he will be walking politely beside you without pulling on the lead. At first, the training sessions should be kept short and very positive; soon the dog will be able to walk nicely with you for increasingly longer distances. Remember also to give the dog free time and the opportunity to run and play when you are done with heel practice.

WEANING OFF FOOD IN TRAINING

Food is used in training new behaviours. Once the dog understands what behaviour goes with a specific command, it is time to start weaning him off the food treats. At first, give a treat after each exercise. Then, start to give a treat only after every other exercise. Mix up the times when you offer a food reward and the times when you only offer praise so that the dog will never know when he is going to receive both food and praise and when he is going to receive only praise. This is called a variable ratio reward system and it proves successful because there is always the chance that the owner will produce a treat, so the dog never stops trying for that reward. No matter what, ALWAYS give verbal praise.

OBEDIENCE CLASSES

It is a good idea to enrol in an obedience class if one is available in your area. If yours is a show dog, ringcraft classes would be more appropriate. Many areas have dog clubs that offer basic obedience training as well as preparatory classes for obedience competition. There are also local dog trainers who offer similar classes.

At obedience trials, dogs can earn titles at various levels of competition. The beginning levels of competition include basic behaviours such as sit, down, heel, etc. The more advanced levels of competition include jumping, retrieving, scent discrimination and signal work. The advanced levels require a dog and owner to put a lot of time and effort into their training and the titles that can be earned at these levels of competition are very prestigious.

OTHER ACTIVITIES FOR LIFE

Whether a dog is trained in the structured environment of a class or alone with his owner at home, there are many activities that can bring fun and rewards to both owner and dog once they have mastered basic control.

Teaching the dog to help out around the home, in the garden or on the farm provides great satisfaction to both dog and owner. In addition, the dog's help makes life a little easier for his owner and raises his stature as a valued companion to his family. It helps

> ## Training Tip
>
> If you are walking your dog and he suddenly stops and looks straight into your eyes, ignore him. Pull the leash and lead him into the direction you want to walk.

give the dog a purpose by occupying his mind and providing an outlet for his energy.

Hiking is an exciting and healthy activity that the dog can be taught without assistance from more than his owner. The exercise of walking and climbing is good for man and dog alike, and the bond that they develop together is priceless.

If you are interested in participating in organised competition with your Bichon, there are activities other than obedience in which you and your dog can become involved. Agility is a popular and fun sport where dogs run through an obstacle course that includes various jumps, tunnels and other exercises to test the dog's speed and coordination. The owners run through the course beside their dogs to give commands and to guide them through the course. Although competitive, the focus is on fun—it's fun to do, fun to watch and great exercise.

Agility competition is fun for dogs of all sizes. The easily trainable Bichon often excels in agility and has a lot of fun with it as well.

109

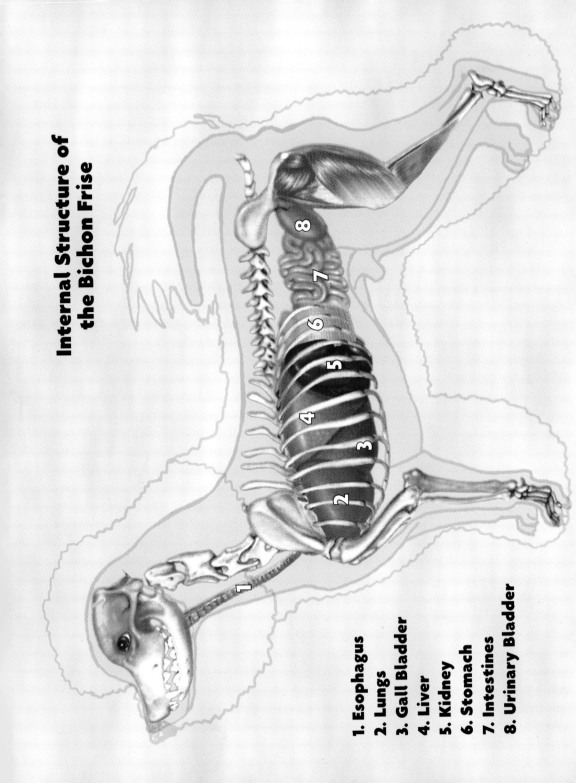

Internal Structure of
the Bichon Frise

1. Esophagus
2. Lungs
3. Gall Bladder
4. Liver
5. Kidney
6. Stomach
7. Intestines
8. Urinary Bladder

Dogs suffer many of the same physical illnesses as people. They might even share many of the same psychological problems. Since people usually know more about human diseases than canine maladies, many of the terms used in this chapter will be familiar but not necessarily those used by veterinary surgeons. We will use the term *x-ray*, instead of the more acceptable term *radiograph*. We will also use the familiar term *symptoms*. Even though dogs don't have symptoms, which are verbal descriptions of the patient's feelings, dogs have *clinical signs*. Since dogs can't speak, we have to look for clinical signs...but we still use the term symptoms in this book.

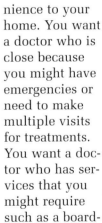

As a general rule, medicine is practised. That term is not arbitrary. Medicine is a constantly changing art as we learn more and more about genetics, electronic aids (like CAT scans) and daily laboratory advances. There are many dog maladies, like canine hip dysplasia, which are not universally treated in the same manner. Some veterinary surgeons opt for surgery more often than others do.

SELECTING A VETERINARY SURGEON
Your selection of a veterinary surgeon should not be based upon personality (as most are) but upon their convenience to your home. You want a doctor who is close because you might have emergencies or need to make multiple visits for treatments. You want a doctor who has services that you might require such as a boarding kennel and grooming facilities, as well as pet supplies and a good reputation for ability and responsiveness. There is nothing more frustrating than having to wait a day or more to get a response from your veterinary surgeon.

A typical American vet's income categorised according to services performed. This survey dealt with small-animal (pet) practices.

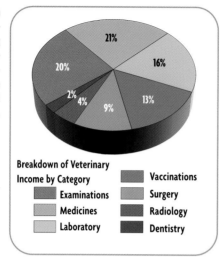

Breakdown of Veterinary Income by Category

- Examinations
- Medicines
- Laboratory
- Vaccinations
- Surgery
- Radiology
- Dentistry

All veterinary surgeons are licensed and their diplomas and/or certificates should be displayed in their waiting rooms. There are, however, many veterinary specialties that usually require further studies and internships. There are specialists in heart problems (veterinary cardiologists), skin problems (veterinary dermatologists), teeth and gum problems (veterinary dentists), eye problems (veterinary ophthalmologists), X-rays (veterinary radiologists), and surgeons who have specialities in bones, muscles or other organs. Most veterinary surgeons do routine surgery such as neutering, stitching up wounds and docking tails for those breeds in which such is required for show purposes. When the problem affecting your dog is serious, it is not unusual or impu-

dent to get another medical opinion, although in Britain you are obliged to advise the vets concerned about this. You might also want to compare costs amongst several veterinary surgeons. Sophisticated health care and veterinary services can be very costly. Don't be bashful about discussing these costs with your veterinary surgeon or his (her) staff. It is not infrequent that important decisions are based upon financial considerations.

PREVENTATIVE MEDICINE
It is much easier, less costly and more effective to practise preventative medicine than to fight bouts of illness and disease. Properly bred puppies come from parents that were selected based upon their genetic disease profile. Their mothers should have been vaccinated, free of all internal and external parasites, and properly nourished. For these reasons, a visit to the veterinary surgeon who cared for the dam (mother) is recommended. The dam can pass on disease resistance to her puppies, which can last for eight to ten weeks. She can also pass on parasites and many infections. That's why you should visit the veterinary surgeon who cared for the dam.

WEANING TO FIVE MONTHS OLD
Puppies should be weaned by the time they are about two months

First Aid
at a Glance

Burns
Place the affected area under cool water;
use ice if only a small area is burnt.

Bee/Insect bites
Apply ice to relieve swelling; antihistamine dosed properly.

Animal bites
Clean any bleeding area; apply pressure until bleeding subsides; go to the vet.

Spider bites
Use cold compress and a pressurised pack to inhibit venom's spreading.

Antifreeze poisoning
Immediately induce vomiting by using hydrogen peroxide.

Fish hooks
Removal best handled by vet;
hook must be cut in order to remove.

Snake bites
Pack ice around bite; contact vet quickly; identify snake for proper antivenin.

Car accident
Move dog from roadway with blanket;
seek veterinary aid.

Shock
Calm the dog, keep him warm; seek immediate veterinary help.

Nosebleed
Apply cold compress to the nose; apply pressure to any visible abrasion.

Bleeding
Apply pressure above the area; treat wound by applying a cotton pack.

Heat stroke
Submerge dog in cold bath; cool down with fresh air and water; go to the vet.

Frostbite/Hypothermia
Warm the dog with a warm bath, electric blankets or hot water bottles.

Abrasions
Clean the wound and wash out thoroughly with fresh water;
apply antiseptic.

 *Remember: an injured dog may attempt
to bite a helping hand from fear and confusion.
Always muzzle the dog before trying to offer assistance.*

old. A puppy that remains for at least eight weeks with its mother and littermates usually adapts better to other dogs and people later in its life.

Some new owners have their puppy examined by a veterinary surgeon immediately, which is a good idea. Vaccination programmes usually begin when the puppy is very young.

The puppy will have its teeth examined and have its skeletal conformation and general health checked prior to certification by the veterinary surgeon. Puppies in certain breeds have problems with their kneecaps, eye cataracts and other eye problems, heart murmurs and undescended testicles. They may also have personality problems and your veterinary surgeon

might have training in temperament evaluation.

VACCINATION SCHEDULING

Most vaccinations are given by injection and should only be done by a veterinary surgeon. Both he and you should keep a record of the date of the injection, the identification of the vaccine and the amount given. Some vets give a first vaccination at eight weeks, but most dog breeders prefer the course not to commence until about ten weeks because of negating any antibodies passed on by the dam. The vaccination scheduling is usually based on a 15-day cycle. You must take your vet's advice as to when to vaccinate as this may differ according to the vaccine used. Most vaccinations immunise your puppy against viruses.

The usual vaccines contain immunising doses of several different viruses such as distemper, parvovirus, parainfluenza and hepatitis. There are other vac-

Normal Skeletal Structure of the Bichon Frise

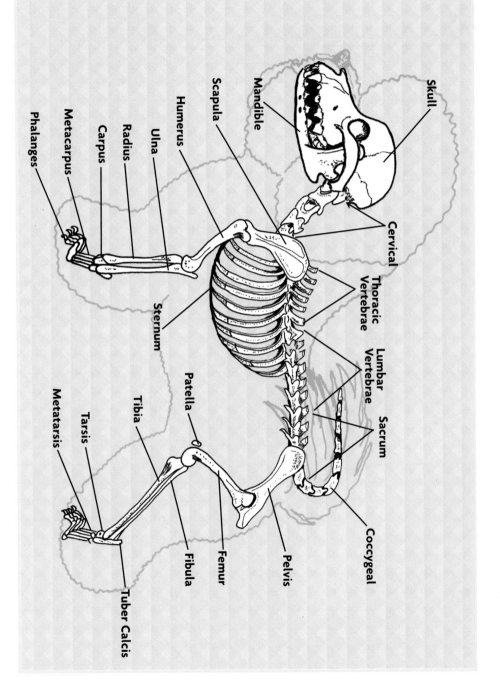

HEALTH AND VACCINATION SCHEDULE

AGE IN WEEKS:	3RD	6TH	8TH	10TH	12TH	14TH	16TH	20-24TH
Worm Control	✔	✔	✔	✔	✔	✔	✔	✔
Neutering								✔
Heartworm*		✔						✔
Parvovirus		✔		✔		✔		✔
Distemper			✔		✔		✔	
Hepatitis			✔		✔		✔	
Leptospirosis		✔		✔		✔		
Parainfluenza		✔		✔		✔		
Dental Examination			✔					✔
Complete Physical			✔					✔
Temperament Testing			✔					
Coronavirus					✔			
Kennel Cough		✔						
Hip Dysplasia							✔	
Rabies*								✔

Vaccinations are not instantly effective. It takes about two weeks for the dog's immunisation system to develop antibodies. Most vaccinations require annual booster shots. Your veterinary surgeon should guide you in this regard.
*Not applicable in the United Kingdom

cines available when the puppy is at risk. You should rely upon professional advice. This is especially true for the booster-shot programme. Most vaccina-tion programmes require a booster when the puppy is a year old and once a year thereafter. In some cases, circumstances may require more frequent immunisations. Kennel cough, more formally known as tracheobronchitis, is treated with a vaccine that is sprayed into the dog's nostrils. Kennel cough is usually included in routine vaccination, but this is often not so effective as for other major diseases.

FIVE MONTHS TO ONE YEAR OF AGE
Unless you intend to breed or

Did You Know?

Not every dog's ears are the same. Ears that are open to the air are healthier than ears with poor air circulation. Sometimes a dog can have two differently shaped ears. You should not probe inside your dog's ears. Only clean that which is accessible with a soft cotton wipe.

show your dog, neutering the puppy at six months of age is recommended. Discuss this with your veterinary surgeon; most professionals advise neutering the puppy. Neutering and spaying are routine procedures, and the best option for pet dogs of both sexes. Neutering has proven to be extremely beneficial to both male and female puppies. Besides eliminating the possibility of pregnancy, it inhibits (but does not prevent) breast cancer in bitches and prostate cancer in male dogs. Under no circumstances should a bitch be spayed prior to her first season.

Did You Know?

Vaccines do not work all the time. Sometimes dogs are allergic to them and many times the antibodies, which are supposed to be stimulated by the vaccine, just are not produced. You should keep your dog in the veterinary clinic for an hour after it is vaccinated to be sure there are no allergic reactions.

DOGS OLDER THAN ONE YEAR
Continue to visit the veterinary surgeon at least once a year. There is no such disease as old age, but bodily functions do change with age. The eyes and ears are no

Disease	What is it?	What causes it?	Symptoms
Leptospirosis	Severe disease that affects the internal organs; can be spread to people.	A bacterium, which is often carried by rodents, that enters through mucous membranes and spreads quickly throughout the body.	Range from fever, vomiting and loss of appetite in less severe cases to shock, irreversible kidney damage and possibly death in most severe cases.
Rabies	Potentially deadly virus that infects warm-blooded mammals. Not seen in United Kingdom.	Bite from a carrier of the virus, mainly wild animals.	1st stage: dog exhibits change in behaviour, fear. 2nd stage: dog's behaviour becomes more aggressive. 3rd stage: loss of coordination, trouble with bodily functions.
Parvovirus	Highly contagious virus, potentially deadly.	Ingestion of the virus, which is usually spread through the faeces of infected dogs.	Most common: severe diarrhoea. Also vomiting, fatigue, lack of appetite.
Kennel cough	Contagious respiratory infection.	Combination of types of bacteria and virus. Most common: *Bordetella bronchiseptica* bacteria and parainfluenza virus.	Chronic cough.
Distemper	Disease primarily affecting respiratory and nervous system.	Virus that is related to the human measles virus.	Mild symptoms such as fever, lack of appetite and mucous secretion progress to evidence of brain damage, 'hard pad.'
Hepatitis	Virus primarily affecting the liver.	Canine adenovirus type I (CAV-1). Enters system when dog breathes in particles.	Lesser symptoms include listlessness, diarrhoea, vomiting. More severe symptoms include 'blue-eye' (clumps of virus in eye).
Coronavirus	Virus resulting in digestive problems.	Virus is spread through infected dog's faeces.	Stomach upset evidenced by lack of appetite, vomiting, diarrhoea.

longer as efficient. Liver, kidney and intestinal functions often decline. Proper dietary changes, recommended by your veterinary surgeon, can make life more pleasant for the ageing Bichon Frise and you.

SKIN PROBLEMS IN BICHONS FRISES

Veterinary surgeons are consulted by dog owners for skin problems more than any other group of diseases or maladies. Dogs' skin is almost as sensitive as human skin and both suffer almost the same ailments. (Though the occurrence of acne in dogs is rare!) For this reason, veterinary dermatology has developed into a speciality practised by many veterinary surgeons.

Since many skin problems have visual symptoms that are almost identical, it requires the skill of an experienced veterinary dermatologist to identify and cure many of the more severe skin disorders. Pet shops

Did You Know?

Your veterinary surgeon will probably recommend that your puppy be vaccinated before you take him outside. There are airborne diseases, parasite eggs in the grass and unexpected visits from other dogs that might be dangerous to your puppy's health.

Health Tip

A dental examination is in order when the dog is between six months and one year of age so any permanent teeth that have erupted incorrectly can be corrected. It is important to begin a brushing routine, preferably using a two-sided brushing technique, whereby both sides of the tooth are brushed at the same time. Durable nylon and safe edible chews should be a part of your puppy's arsenal for good health, good teeth and pleasant breath. The vast majority of dogs three to four years old and older has diseases of their gums from lack of dental attention. Using the various types of dental chews can be very effective in controlling dental plaque.

sell many treatments for skin problems but most of the treatments are directed at symptoms and not the underlying problem(s). If your dog is suffering from a skin disorder, you should seek professional assistance as quickly as possible. As with all diseases, the earlier a problem is identified and treated, the more successful is the cure.

INHERITED SKIN PROBLEMS

Many skin disorders are inherited and some are fatal. For example,

Acrodermatitis is an inherited disease that is transmitted by both parents. The parents, who appear (phenotypically) normal, have a recessive gene for acrodermatitis, meaning that they carry, but are not affected by the disease.

Acrodermatitis is just one example of how difficult it is to prevent congenital dog diseases. The cost and skills required to ascertain whether two dogs should be mated are too high even though puppies with acrodermatitis rarely reach two years of age.

Other inherited skin problems are usually not as fatal as acrodermatitis. All inherited diseases must be diagnosed and treated by a veterinary specialist. There are active programmes being undertaken by many veterinary pharmaceutical manufacturers to solve most, if not all, of the common skin problems of dogs.

PARASITE BITES

Many of us are allergic to insect bites. The bites itch, erupt and may even become infected. Dogs have the same reaction to fleas,

Acrodermatitis

There is a 25% chance of a puppy getting this fatal gene combination from two parents with recessive genes for acrodermatitis:

AA= NORMAL, HEALTHY
aa= FATAL
Aa= RECESSIVE, NORMAL APPEARING

If the female parent has an Aa gene and the male parent has an Aa gene, the chances are one in four that the puppy will have the fatal genetic combination aa.

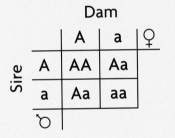

		Dam		
		A	a	♀
Sire	A	AA	Aa	
	a	Aa	aa	
	♂			

Did You Know?

Feeding your dog properly is very important. An incorrect diet could affect the dog's health, behaviour and nervous system, possibly making a normal dog into an aggressive one.

ticks and/or mites. When an insect lands on you, you have the chance to whisk it away with your hand. Unfortunately, when our dog is bitten by a flea, tick or mite, it can only scratch it away or bite it. By the time the dog has been bitten, the parasite has done some of its damage. It may also have laid eggs to cause further problems in the near future. The itching from parasite bites is probably due to the saliva injected into the site when the parasite sucks the dog's blood.

AUTO-IMMUNE SKIN CONDITIONS

Auto-immune skin conditions are commonly referred to as being allergic to yourself, whilst allergies are usually inflammatory reactions to an outside stimulus. Auto-immune diseases cause serious damage to the tissues that are involved.

The best known auto-immune disease is lupus, which affects people as well as dogs. The symptoms are variable and may affect the kidneys, bones, blood chemistry and skin. It can be fatal to both dogs and humans, though it is not thought to be transmissible. It is usually successfully treated with cortisone, prednisone or similar corticosteroid, but extensive use of these drugs can have harmful side effects.

AIRBORNE ALLERGIES

An interesting allergy is pollen allergy. Humans have hay fever, rose fever and other fevers with which they suffer during the pollinating season. Many dogs suffer the same allergies. When the pollen count is high, your dog might suffer but don't expect them to sneeze and have runny noses like humans. Dogs react to pollen allergies the same way they react to fleas—they scratch and bite themselves.

Dogs, like humans, can be tested for allergens. Discuss the testing with your veterinary dermatologist.

FOOD PROBLEMS
FOOD ALLERGIES

Dogs are allergic to many foods that are best-sellers and highly recommended by breeders and veterinary surgeons. Changing the brand of food that you buy may not eliminate the problem if the element to which the dog is allergic is contained in the new brand.

Recognising a food allergy is difficult. Humans vomit or have rashes when they eat a food to which they are allergic. Dogs neither vomit nor (usually) develop a rash. They react in the same manner as they do to an airborne or flea allergy: they itch, scratch and bite. Thus making the diagnosis extremely difficult. Whilst pollen allergies and parasite bites are usually seasonal, food allergies are year-round problems.

FOOD INTOLERANCE

Food intolerance is the inability of the dog to completely digest certain foods. Puppies that may have done very well on their mother's milk may not do well on cow's milk. The result of this food intolerance may be loose bowels, passing gas and stomach pains. These are the only obvious symptoms of food intolerance and that makes diagnosis difficult.

TREATING FOOD PROBLEMS

It is possible to handle food allergies and food intolerance yourself. Put your dog on a diet that it has never had. Obviously if it has never eaten this new food it can't have been allergic or intolerant of it. Start with a single ingredient that is not in the dog's diet at the present time. Ingredients like chopped beef or fish are common in dog's diets, so try something more exotic like rabbit, pheasant or even just vegetables. Keep the dog on this diet (with no addi-

tives) for a month. If the symptoms of food allergy or intolerance disappear, chances are your dog has a food allergy.

Don't think that the single ingredient cured the problem. You still must find a suitable diet and ascertain which ingredient in the old diet was objectionable. This is most easily done by adding ingredients to the new diet one at a time. Let the dog stay on the modified diet for a month before you add another ingredient. Eventually, you will determine the ingredient that caused the adverse reaction.

An alternative method is to carefully study the ingredients in the diet to which your dog is allergic or intolerable. Identify the main ingredient in this diet and eliminate the main ingredient by buying a different food that does not have that ingredient. Keep experimenting until the symptoms disappear after one month on the new diet.

Did You Know?

The myth that dogs need extra fat in their diets can be harmful. Should your vet recommend extra fat, use safflower oil instead of animal oils. Safflower oil has been shown to be less likely to cause allergic reactions.

121

EXTERNAL PARASITES

Of all the problems to which dogs are prone, none is more well known and frustrating than fleas. Fleas, which usually refers to fleas, ticks and mites, are difficult to prevent but relatively simple to cure. Parasites that are harboured inside the body are more difficult to cure but they are easier to control.

FLEAS

To control a flea infestation you have to understand the life cycle of a typical flea. Fleas are often thought of as a summertime prob-

lem but centrally heated homes have rather changed the pattern and fleas can be found at any time of the year. There is no single flea-control medicine (insecticide) that can be used in every flea-infested area. To understand flea control you must apply suitable treatment to the weak link in the life cycle of the flea.

THE LIFE CYCLE OF A FLEA

Fleas are found in four forms: eggs, larvae, pupae and adults. You really need a low-power microscope or hand lens to identify a living flea's eggs, pupae or larvae. They spend their whole lives on your Bichon Frise unless they are forcibly removed by brushing, bathing, scratching or biting.

The dog flea is scientifically known as *Ctenocephalides canis* whilst the cat flea is *Ctenocephalides felis*. Several species infest both dog and cats.

Fleas lay eggs whilst they are in residence upon your dog.

Did You Know?

Flea-killers are poisonous. You should not spray these toxic chemicals on areas of the dog's body that he licks, on his genitals or on his face. Flea-killers taken internally are a better answer, but check with your vet in case internal therapy is not advised for your dog.

These eggs fall off almost as soon as they dry (they may be a bit damp when initially laid) and are the reservoir of future flea infestations. If your dog scratches himself and is able to dislodge a few fleas, they simply fall off and await a future chance to attack a dog...or even a person. Yes, fleas from dogs bite people. That's why it is so important to control fleas both on the dog and in the dog's entire environment. You must, therefore, treat the dog and the environment simultaneously.

S.E.M. BY DR. DENNIS KUNKEL, UNIVERSITY OF HAWAII.

DE-FLEAING THE HOME

Cleanliness is the simple rule. If you have a cat living with your dog, the matter is more complicated since most dog fleas are actually cat fleas. Cats climb onto many areas that are never accessible to dogs (like window sills, table tops, etc.), so you have to clean all

On Guard: Catching Fleas Off Guard

Consider the following ways to arm yourself against fleas:

• Add a small amount of pennyroyal or eucalyptus oil to your dog's bath. These natural remedies repel fleas.

• Supplement your dog's food with fresh garlic (minced or grated) and a hearty amount of brewer's yeast, both of which ward off fleas.

• Use a flea comb on your dog daily. Submerge fleas in a cup of bleach to kill them quickly.

• Confine the dog to only a few rooms to limit the spread of fleas in the home.

• Vacuum daily...and get all of the crevices! Dispose of the bag every few days until the problem is under control.

• Nematodes are microscopic worms that eat flea larvae and pupae. Spray them on damp areas, which fleas love. Once the fleas have been eaten, the worms will vanish, too.

• Wash your dog's bedding daily. Cover cushions where your dog sleeps with towels, and wash the towels often.

• Throw away your dog's flea collars. They are a waste of money and do not work!

A scanning eletron microhraph (S.E.M.) of a dog flea, *Ctenocephalides canis*.

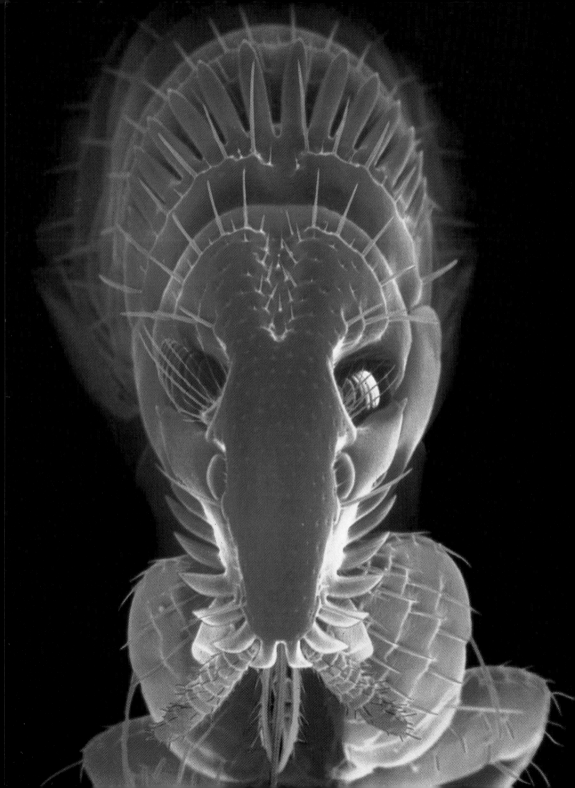

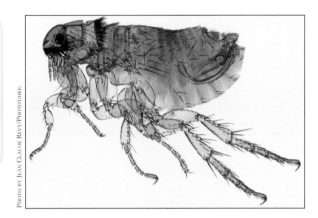

PHOTO BY JEAN CLAUDE REVY/PHOTOTAKE.

A male dog flea, *Ctenocephalides canis*.

of these areas. The hard floor surfaces (tiles, wood, stone and linoleum) must be mopped several times a day. Drops of food onto the floor are actually food for flea larvae! All rugs and furniture must be vacuumed several times a day. Don't forget cupboards, under furniture and cushions. A study has reported that a vacuum cleaner with a beater bar can remove only 20% of the larvae and 50% of the eggs. The vacuum bags should be discarded into a sealed plastic bag or burned. The vacuum machine itself should be cleaned. The outdoor area to which your dog has access must also be treated with an insecticide.

Your vet will be able to recommend a household insecticidal spray but this must be used with caution and instructions strictly followed.

Opposite page: A scanning eletron micrograph (S.E.M.) of a dog or cat flea, *Ctenocephalides*. This has been coloured for effect.

There are many drugs available to kill fleas on the dog itself, such as the miracle drug ivermectin, and it is best to have the de-fleaing and de-worming supervised by your vet. Ivermectin is

A male cat flea *Ctenocephalides felis*. Cat fleas are very commonly found on dogs.

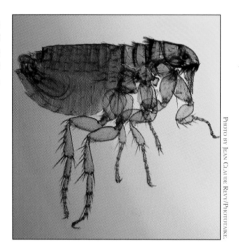

PHOTO BY JEAN CLAUDE REVY/PHOTOTAKE

Dwight R. Kuhn's magnificent action photo showing a flea jumping from a dog's back.

effective against many external and internal parasites including heartworms, roundworms, tapeworms, flukes, ticks and mites. It has not been approved for use to control these pests, but veterinary surgeons frequently use it anyway. Ivermectin may not be available in all areas.

STERILISING THE ENVIRONMENT
Besides cleaning your home with vacuum cleaners and mops, you have to treat the outdoor range of your dog. When trimming bushes and spreading insecticide, be careful not to poison areas in which fishes or other animals reside.

TICKS AND MITES
Though not as common as fleas, ticks and mites are found all over the tropical and temperate world. They don't bite like fleas, they harpoon. They dig their sharp proboscis (nose) into the dog's skin and drink the blood, which is their only food and drink. Dogs can get paralysis, Lyme disease, Rocky Mountain spotted fever (normally found in the U.S.A. only), and many other diseases from ticks and mites. They may live where fleas are found but they also like to hide in cracks or seams in walls wherever dogs live. They are controlled the same way fleas are controlled.

The tick *Dermacentor variabilis* may well be the most common dog tick in many geographi-

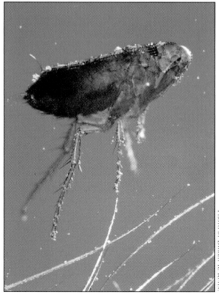

PHOTO BY DWIGHT R. KUHN.

The Life Cycle of the Flea

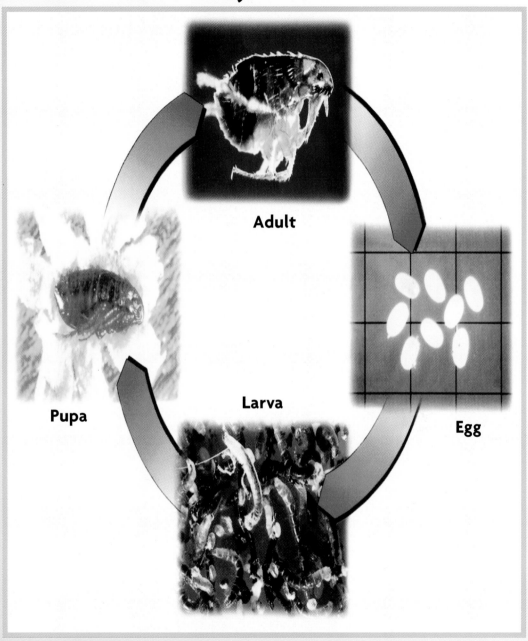

Adult

Pupa

Larva

Egg

The eggs of the dog flea magnified.

cal areas, especially where the climate is hot and humid.

Most dog ticks have life expectancies of a week to six months, depending upon climatic conditions. They neither jump nor fly, but crawl slowly and can range up to 5 metres (16 feet) to reach a sleeping or unsuspecting dog.

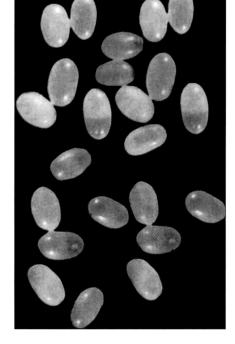

Did You Know?

Two types of products should be used when treating fleas—a product to treat the pet and a product to treat the home. Adult fleas represent less than 1% of the flea population. The pre-adult fleas (eggs, larvae and pupae) represent more than 99% of the flea population and are found in the environment; it is in the case of pre-adult fleas that products containing an Insect Growth Regulator (IGR) should be used in the home. IGRs are a new class of compounds used to prevent the development of insects. They do not kill the insect outright, but instead use the insect's biology against it to stop it from completing its growth. Products that contain methoprene are the world's first and leading IGRs. Used to control fleas and other insects, this type of IGR will stop flea larvae from developing and protect the house for up to seven months.

MANGE

Mange is a skin irritation caused by mites. Some mites are contagious, like *Cheyletiella*, ear mites, scabies and chiggers. The non-contagious mites are *Demodex*. The most serious of the mites is the one that causes ear-mite infestation. Ear mites are usually controlled with ivermectin.

It is essential that your dog be treated for mange as quickly as possible because some forms of mange are transmissible to people.

INTERNAL PARASITES

Most animals—fishes, birds and mammals, including dogs and humans—have worms and other parasites that live inside their bodies. According to Dr Herbert R Axelrod, the fish pathologist, there are two kinds of parasites: dumb and smart. The smart parasites live in peaceful cooperation with their hosts (symbiosis), whilst the dumb parasites kill their host. Most of the worm

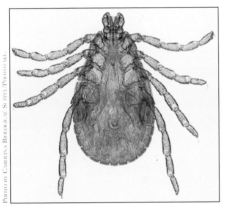

Above: Magnified head of a dog flea, *Cteno-cephalides canis.* Left: A brown dog tick, *Rhipi-cephalus sanguineus,* is an uncommon but annoying tick found on dogs. Below: Human lice look like dog lice; the two are closely related.

infections are relatively easy to control. If they are not controlled they eventually weaken the host dog to the point that other medical problems occur, but they are not dumb parasites that directly cause the death of their hosts.

ROUNDWORMS

The roundworms that infect dogs are scientifically known as *Toxocara canis.* They live in the dog's intestine and shed eggs continually. It has been estimated that an average-sized dog produces about 150 grammes of faeces every day. Each gramme of faeces averages

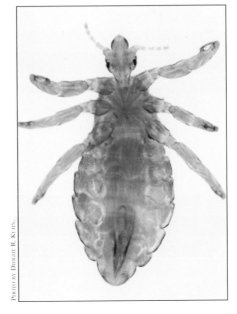

129

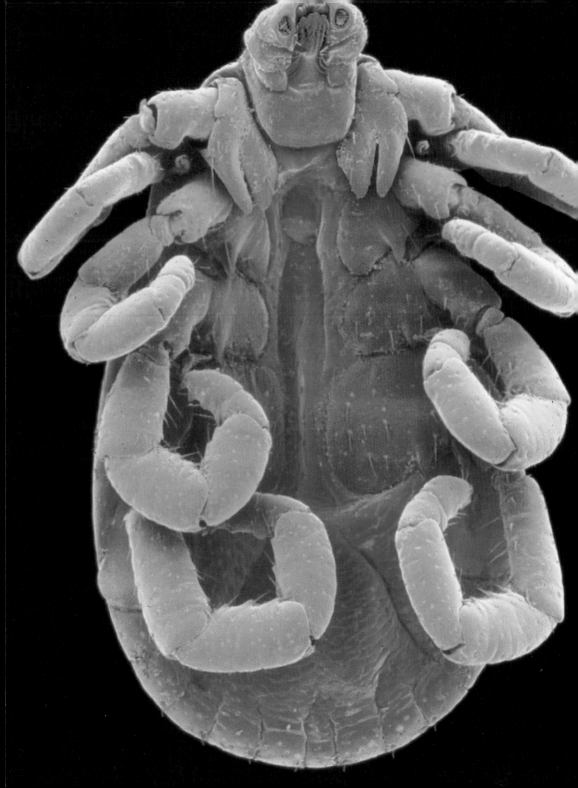

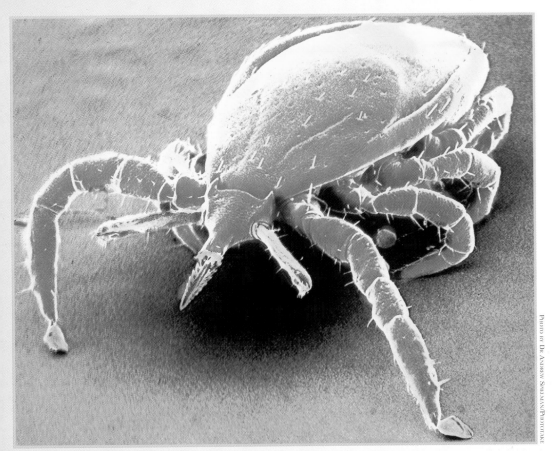

Photo by Dr. Andrew Spielman/Phototake

A deer tick, the carrier of Lyme disease.

Opposite page:
The dog tick,
*Dermacentor vari-
abilis*, is probably
the most common
tick found on
dogs. Look at the
strength in its
eight legs! No
wonder it's hard to
detach them.

An uncommon
dog tick of the
genus *Ixode*.
Magnified 10x.

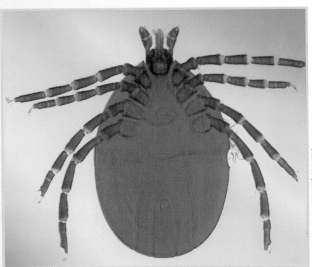

Photo by Jean Claude Revy/Phototake

The dog mange mite is frequently seen on cows as well.

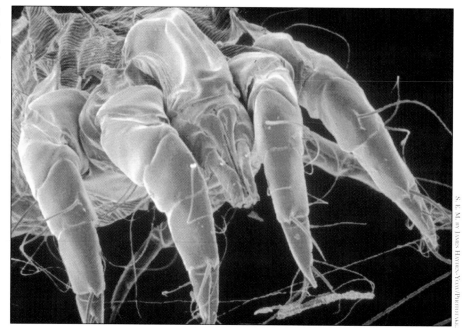

S. E. M. by James Hawkes-Yonv/Phototake

Magnified view of the mange mite, *Psoroptes bovis.*

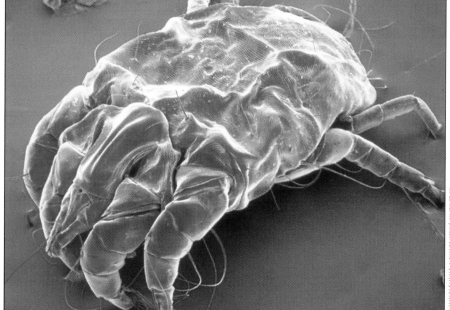

S. E. M. by James Hawkes-Yonv/Phototake

It changes the site of its attachment about six times a day, and the dog loses blood from each detachment. This blood loss can cause iron-deficiency anaemia. Hookworms are easily purged from the dog with many medications, the best of which seems to be ivermectin even though it has not been approved for such use.

In Britain, the 'temperate climate' hookworm (*Uncinaria stenocephala*) is rarely found in

The head of the dog tick, *Derma-centor variabilis*.

10,000–12,000 eggs of roundworms. All areas in which dogs roam contain astronomical numbers of roundworm eggs. The greatest danger of roundworms is that they infect people, too! It is wise to have your dog tested regularly for roundworms.

Pigs also have roundworm infections that can be passed to human and dogs. The typical pig roundworm parasite is called *Ascaris lumbricoides*.

HOOKWORMS

The worm *Ancylostoma caninum* is commonly called the dog hookworm. It is also dangerous to humans and cats. It attaches itself to the dog's intestines by its teeth.

Did You Know?

Ridding your puppy of worms is VERY IMPORTANT because certain worms that puppies carry, such as tapeworms and roundworms, can infect humans.

Breeders initiate a deworming programme at or about four weeks of age. The routine is repeated every two or three weeks until the puppy is three months old. The breeder from whom you obtained your puppy should provide you with the complete details of the deworming programme.

Your veterinary surgeon can prescribe and monitor the programme of deworming for you. The usual programme is treating the puppy every 15–20 days until the puppy is positively worm free.

It is not advised that you treat your puppy with drugs that are not recommended professionally.

133

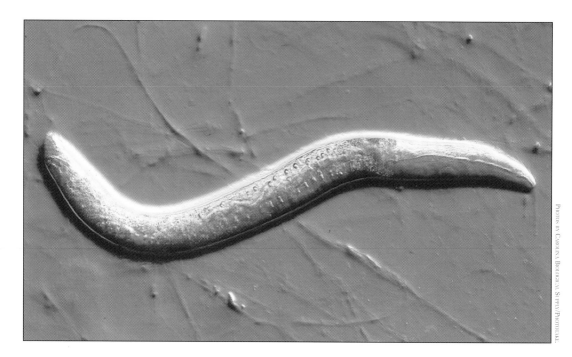

Two views of the roundworm, *Rhabditis*. The roundworm can infect both dogs and humans.

pet or show dogs, but can occur in hunting packs, racing Greyhounds and sheepdogs because these hookworms can be prevalent wherever dogs are exercised regularly on grassland.

Did You Know?

Humans, rats, squirrels, foxes, coyotes, wolves, mixed breeds of dogs and purebred dogs are all susceptible to tapeworm infection. Except in humans, tapeworms are usually not a fatal infection.

Infected individuals can harbour a thousand parasitic worms.

Tapeworms have two sexes—male and female (many other worms have only one sex—male and female in the same worm).

If dogs eat infected rats or mice, they get the tapeworm disease.

One month after attaching to a dog's intestine, the worm starts shedding eggs. These eggs are infective immediately.

Infective eggs can live for a few months without a host animal.

Roundworms, whipworms and tapeworms are just a few of the other commonly known worms that infect dogs.

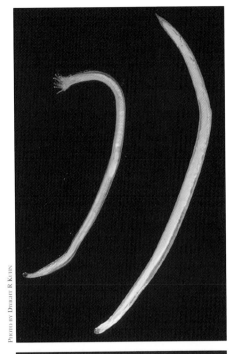

PHOTO BY DWIGHT R KUHN

Male and female hookworms, *Ancylostoma caninum*, are uncommonly found in pet or show dogs in Britain. Hookworms may infect other dogs that have exposure to grasslands.

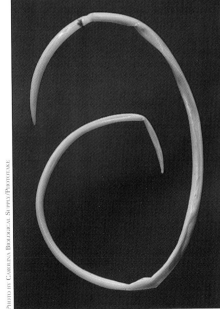

PHOTO BY CAROLINA BIOLOGICAL SUPPLY/PHOTOTAKE

The roundworm *Rhabditis*.

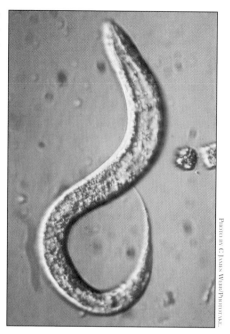

The infective stage of the hookworm larva.

Photo by C James Webb/Phototake

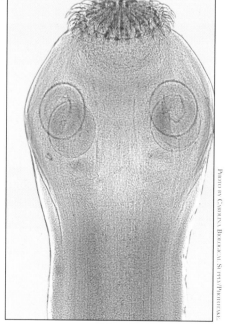

The head and rostellum (the round prominence on the scolex) of a tapeworm, which infects dogs and humans.

Photo by Carolina Biological Supply/Phototake

TAPEWORMS

There are many species of tapeworms, many of which are carried by fleas! The dog eats the flea and starts the tapeworm cycle. Humans can also be infected with tapeworms, so don't eat fleas! Fleas are so small that your dog could pass them onto your hands, your plate or your food and make it possible for you to ingest a flea which is carrying tapeworm eggs.

Whilst tapeworm infection is not life threatening in dogs (smart parasite!), it can be the cause of a very serious liver disease for

Did You Know?

Average size dogs can pass 1,360,000 roundworm eggs every day.

For example, if there were only 1 million dogs in the world, the world would be saturated with 1,300 metric tonnes of dog faeces.

These faeces would contain 15,000,000,000 roundworm eggs.

7–31% of home gardens and children's play boxes in the U. S. contained roundworm eggs.

Flushing dog's faeces down the toilet is not a safe practice because the usual sewage treatments do not destroy roundworm eggs.

Infected puppies start shedding roundworm eggs at 3 weeks of age. They can be infected by their mother's milk.

humans. About 50 percent of the humans infected with *Echinococcus multilocularis*, causing alveolar hydatis, perish.

HEARTWORMS

Heartworms are thin, extended worms up to 30 cms (12 ins) long that live in a dog's heart and the

Did You Know?

It was announced in April 1999 that the severe quarantine laws imposed on animals entering Britain from other rabies-free countries would become a thing of the past by April 2001. Rather than being confined to a kennel for six months upon arrival in Britain, animals undergo a series of blood tests and vaccinations, and are identifed by microchip implantation. Qualified pets receive a 'health passport' that allows their owners to travel with them in between Britain and other (mostly European) countries in which rabies does not exist.

Animals from countries such as the United States and Canada, where rabies is a problem, still will be subject to quarantine. Although veterinary standards are high in these countries, recently infected dogs may test negative to the disease and, without the quarantine period, may unknowingly introduce rabies into previously unaffected countries.

Did You Know?

Never allow your dog to swim in polluted water or public areas where water quality can be suspect. Even perfectly clear water can harbour parasites, many of which can cause serious to fatal illnesses in canines. Areas inhabited by waterfowl and other wildlife are especially dangerous.

major blood vessels around it. Bichons Frises may have up to 200 of these worms. The symptoms may be loss of energy, loss of appetite, coughing, the development of a pot belly and anaemia.

Heartworms are transmitted by mosquitoes. The mosquito drinks the blood of an infected dog and takes in larvae with the blood. The larvae, called microfilaria, develop within the body of the mosquito and are passed on to the next dog bitten after the larvae mature. It takes two to three weeks for the larvae to develop to the infective stage within the body of the mosquito. Dogs should be treated at about six weeks of age, then every six months.

Blood testing for heartworms is not necessarily indicative of how seriously your dog is infected. This is a dangerous disease. Although heartworm affects dogs in America, Asia, Australia, and Central Europe, dogs in Britain are not affected by heartworm.

137

The heartworm, *Dirofilaria immitis.*

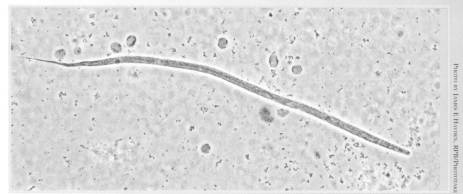

Magnified heartworm larvae, *Dirofilaria immitis.*

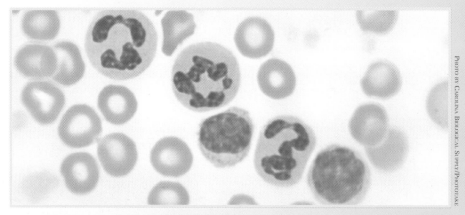

The heart of a dog infected with canine heartworm, *Dirofilaria immitis.*

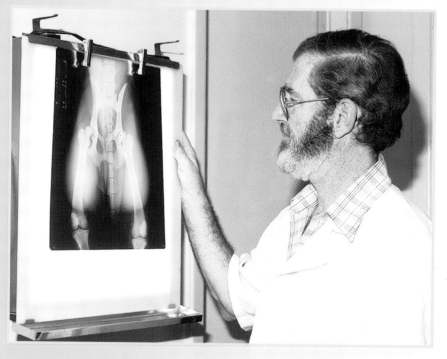

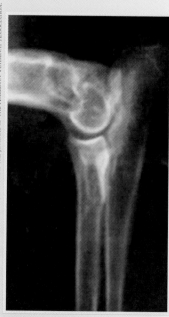

(Above) A veterinary surgeon evaluating a dog's x-ray for hip dysplasia. Diagnosis can only be made using radiographic techniques, which are interpreted (read) by a suitably trained veterinary surgeon.

(Below) The lateral (far left illustration) and flexed lateral (far right illustration) of a three-year-old dog's elbow manifesting elbow dysplasia with associated problems (acute, severe weight-bearing lameness of the right forelimb).

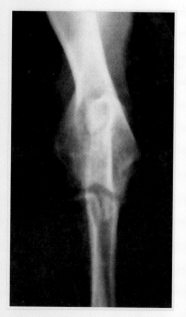

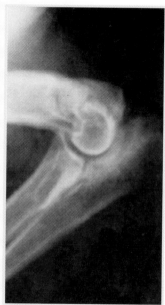

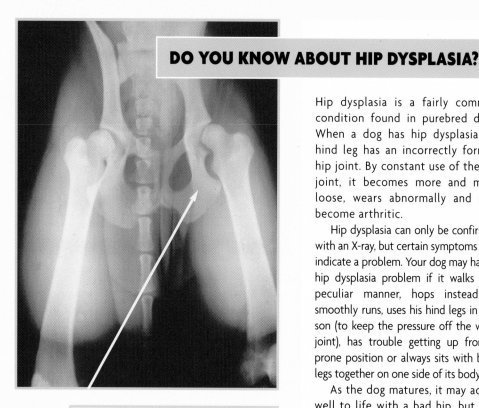

DO YOU KNOW ABOUT HIP DYSPLASIA?

Hip dysplasia is a fairly common condition found in purebred dogs. When a dog has hip dysplasia, its hind leg has an incorrectly formed hip joint. By constant use of the hip joint, it becomes more and more loose, wears abnormally and may become arthritic.

Hip dysplasia can only be confirmed with an X-ray, but certain symptoms may indicate a problem. Your dog may have a hip dysplasia problem if it walks in a peculiar manner, hops instead of smoothly runs, uses his hind legs in unison (to keep the pressure off the weak joint), has trouble getting up from a prone position or always sits with both legs together on one side of its body.

As the dog matures, it may adapt well to life with a bad hip, but in a few years the arthritis develops and many dogs with hip dysplasia become cripples.

Hip dysplasia is considered an inherited disease and can usually be diagnosed when the dog is three to nine months old. Some experts claim that a special diet might help your puppy outgrow the bad hip, but the usual treatments are surgical. The removal of the pectineus muscle, the removal of the round part of the femur, reconstructing the pelvis and replacing the hip with an artificial one are all surgical interventions that are expensive, but they are usually very successful. Follow the advice of your veterinary surgeon.

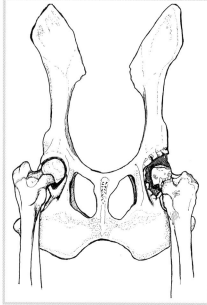

Hip dysplasia is a badly worn hip joint caused by improper fit of the bone into the socket. It is easily the most common hip problem in larger dogs, but dogs of any breed can be affected by hip dysplasia. The illustration shows a healthy hip joint on the left and an unhealthy hip joint on the right.

CDS: COGNITIVE DYSFUNCTION SYNDROME
'Old Dog Syndrome'

There are many ways for you to evaluate old-dog syndrome. Veterinary surgeons have defined CDS (cognitive dysfunction syndrome) as the gradual deterioration of cognitive abilities. These are indicated by changes in the dog's behaviour. When a dog changes its routine response, and maladies have been eliminated as the cause of these behavioural changes, then CDS is the usual diagnosis.

More than half the dogs over 8 years old suffer some form of CDS. The older the dog, the more chance it has of suffering from CDS. In humans, doctors often dismiss the CDS behavioural changes as part of 'winding down.'

There are four major signs of CDS: frequent toilet accidents inside the home, sleeps much more or much less than normal, acts confused, and fails to respond to social stimuli.

SYMPTOMS OF CDS

FREQUENT TOILET ACCIDENTS
- *Urinates in the house.*
- *Defecates in the house.*
- *Doesn't signal that he wants to go out.*

SLEEP PATTERNS
- *Moves much more slowly.*
- *Sleeps more than normal during the day.*
- *Sleeps less during the night.*
- *Walks around listlessly and without a destination goal.*

CONFUSION
- *Goes outside and just stands there.*
- *Appears confused with a faraway look in his eyes.*
- *Hides more often.*
- *Doesn't recognise friends.*
- *Doesn't come when called.*

FAILS TO RESPOND TO SOCIAL STIMULI
- *Comes to people less frequently, whether called or not.*
- *Doesn't tolerate petting for more than a short time.*
- *Doesn't come to the door when you return home from work.*

BICHON FRISE

The term *old* is a qualitative term. For dogs, as well as their masters, old is relative. Certainly we can all distinguish between a puppy Bichon Frise and an adult Bichon Frise—there are the obvious physical traits, such as size, appearance and facial expressions, and personality traits. Puppies that are nasty are very rare. Puppies and young dogs like to play with children. Children's natural exuberance is a good match for the seemingly endless energy of young dogs. They like to run, jump, chase and retrieve. When dogs grow up and cease their interaction with children, they are often thought of as being too old to play with the kids.

On the other hand, if a Bichon Frise is only exposed to people over 60 years of age, its life will normally be less active and it will not seem to be getting old as its activity level slows down.

If people live to be 100 years old, dogs live to be 20 years old. Whilst this is a good rule of thumb, it is very inaccurate. When trying to compare dog years to human years, you cannot make a generalisation about all dogs. You can make the generalisation that 15 years is a good life span for a Bichon Frise, which is quite good compared to, say, a Great Dane. Many large breeds typically live for fewer years than smaller ones. Dogs are generally considered mature within three years, but they can reproduce even earlier. So the first three years of a dog's life are like seven times that of comparable humans. That means a 3-year-old dog is like a 21-year-old human. As the curve of comparison shows, there is no hard and fast rule for comparing dog and human ages. The comparison is made even more difficult, for not all humans age at the same rate...and human females live longer than human males.

WHAT TO LOOK FOR IN SENIORS

Most veterinary surgeons and behaviourists use the seventh year mark as the time to consider a dog a 'senior.' The term 'senior' does not imply that the dog is geriatric and has begun to fail in mind and body. Ageing is essentially a slowing process. Humans readily admit that they feel a difference in their activity level from age 20 to 30, and then from 30 to 40, etc. By treating the seven-year-old dog as a senior, owners are able to implement certain therapeutic and preventive medical strategies with the help of their veterinary surgeons. A senior-care programme should include at least two veterinary visits per year, screening sessions to determine the dog's health status, as well as nutritional counselling. Veterinary surgeons determine the senior dog's health status through a blood smear for a complete blood count, serum chemistry profile with electrolytes, urinalysis, blood pressure check, electrocardiogram, ocular tonometry (pressure on the eyeball) and dental prophylaxis.

Such an extensive programme for senior dogs is well advised before owners start to see the obvious physical signs of ageing,

Did You Know?

An old dog starts to show one or more of the following symptoms:

• The hair on its face and paws starts to turn grey. The colour breakdown usually starts around the eyes and mouth.

• Sleep patterns are deeper and longer and the old dog is harder to awaken.

• Food intake diminishes.

• Responses to calls, whistles and other signals are ignored more and more.

• Eye contacts do not evoke tail wagging (assuming they once did).

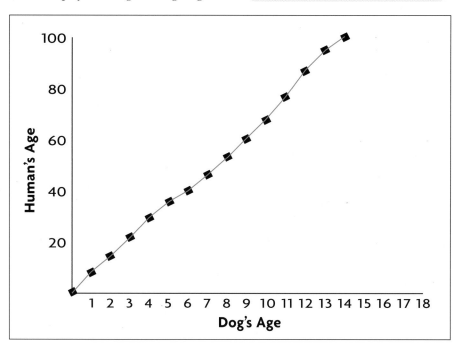

such as slower and inhibited movement, greying, increased sleep/nap periods, and disinterest in play and other activity. This preventative programme promises a longer, healthier life for the ageing dog. Amongst the physical problems common in ageing dogs are the loss of sight and vision, arthritis, kidney and liver failure, diabetes mellitus, heart disease and Cushing's disease (a hormonal disease).

Did You Know?

The symptoms listed below are symptoms that gradually appear and become more noticeable. They are not life threatening, however, the symptoms below are to be taken very seriously and a discussion with your veterinary surgeon is warranted:

• Your dog cries and whimpers when it moves and stops running completely.

• Convulsions start or become more serious and frequent. The usual convulsion (spasm) is when the dog stiffens and starts to tremble being unable or unwilling to move. The seizure usually lasts for 5 to 30 minutes.

• Your dog drinks more water and urinates more frequently. Wetting and bowel accidents take place indoors without warning.

• Vomiting becomes more and more frequent.

In addition to the physical manifestations discussed, there are some behavioural changes and problems related to ageing dogs. Dogs suffering from hearing or vision loss, dental discomfort or arthritis can become aggressive. Likewise the near-deaf and/or blind dog may be startled more easily and react in an unexpectedly aggressive manner. Seniors suffering from senility can become more impatient and irritable. Housesoiling accidents are associated with loss of mobility, kidney problems, loss of sphincter control as well as plaque accumulation, physiological brain changes, and reactions to medications. Older dogs, just like young puppies, suffer from separation anxiety, which can lead to excessive barking, whining, housesoiling, and destructive behaviour. Seniors may become fearful of everyday sounds, such as vacuum cleaners, heaters, thunder, and passing traffic. Some dogs have difficulty sleeping, due to discomfort, the need for frequent potty visits, and the like. Owners should avoid spoiling the older dog with too many fatty treats. Obesity is a common problem in older dogs and subtracts years from their lifespan. Keep the senior dog as trim as possible since excessive weight puts additional stress on the body's vital organs. Some breeders recommend supplementing the diet

When Your Dog Gets Old...
Signs the Owner Can Look For

IF YOU NOTICE...	IT COULD INDICATE...
Discolouration of teeth and gums, foul breath, loss of appetite	Abcesses, gum disease, mouth lesions
Lumps, bumps, cysts, warts, fatty tumours	Cancers, benign or malignant
Cloudiness of eyes, apparent loss of sight	Cataracts, lenticular sclerosis, PRA, retinal dysplasia, blindness
Flaky coat, alopaecia (hair loss)	Hormonal problems, hypothyroidism
Obesity, appetite loss, excessive weight gain	Various problems
Household accidents, increased urination	Diabetes, kidney or bladder disease
Increased thirst	Kidney disease, diabetes mellitus
Change in sleeping habits, coughing	Heart disease
Difficulty moving	Arthritis, degenerative joint disease, spondylosis (degenerative spine disease)

If you notice any of these signs, an appointment should be made immediately with a veterinary surgeon for a thorough evaluation.

DID YOU KNOW?

Your senior dog may lose interest in eating, not because he's less hungry but because his senses of smell and taste have diminished. The old chow simply does not smell as good as it once did. Additionally, older dogs use less energy and thereby can sustain themselves on less food.

he does appreciate the considerations you offer as he gets older.

Your Bichon Frise does not understand why his world is slowing down. Owners must make the transition into the golden years as pleasant and rewarding as possible.

WHAT TO DO WHEN THE TIME COMES

You are never fully prepared to make a rational decision about putting your dog to sleep. It is very obvious that you love your Bichon Frise or you would not be reading this book. Putting a loved dog to sleep is extremely difficult. It is a decision that must be made with your veterinary surgeon. You

with foods high in fibre and lower in calories. Adding fresh vegetables and marrow broth to the senior's diet makes a tasty, low-calorie, low-fat supplement. Vets also offer specialty diets for senior dogs that are worth exploring.

Your dog, as he nears his twilight years, needs his owner's patience and good care more than ever. Never punish an older dog for an accident or abnormal behaviour. For all the years of love, protection and companionship that your dog has provided, he deserves special attention and courtesies. The older dog may need to relieve himself at 3 a.m. because he can no longer hold it for eight hours. Older dogs may not be able to remain crated for more than two or three hours. It may be time to give up a sofa or chair to your old friend. Although he may not seem as enthusiastic about your attention and petting,

A resting place for your dog's ashes may be available locally. Contact you veterinary surgeon or local dog club for information.

are usually forced to make the decision when one of the life-threatening symptoms listed above becomes serious enough for you to seek medical (veterinary) help.

If the prognosis of the malady indicates the end is near and your beloved pet will only suffer more

If you are interested in burying your dog, there are pet cemeteries that cater to pet lovers.

and experience no enjoyment for the balance of its life, then euthanasia is the right choice.

WHAT IS EUTHANASIA?

Euthanasia derives from the Greek meaning *good death*. In other words, it means the planned, painless killing of a dog suffering from a painful, incurable condition, or who is so aged that it cannot walk, see, eat or control its excretory functions.

Euthanasia is usually accomplished by injection with an overdose of an anaesthesia or barbiturate. Aside from the prick of the needle, the experience is usually painless.

HOW ABOUT YOU?

The decision to euthanize your dog is never easy. The days during which the dog becomes ill and the

Did You Know?

The more open discussion you have about the whole stressful occurrence, the easier it will be for you when the time comes.

147

end occurs can be unusually stressful for you. If this is your first experience with the death of a loved one, you may need the comfort dictated by your religious beliefs. If you are the head of the family and have children, you should have involved them in the decision of putting your Bichon Frise to sleep. Usually your dog can be maintained on drugs for a few days in order to give you ample time to make a decision. During this time, talking with members of your family or even people who have lived through this same experience can ease the burden.

THE FINAL RESTING PLACE

Dogs can have some of the same privileges as humans. They can occasionally be buried in their entirety in a pet cemetery which is generally expensive, or if they have died at home can be buried in your garden in a place suitably marked with some stone or newly planted tree or bush. Alternatively they can be cremated and the ashes returned to you, or some people prefer to leave their dogs at the surgery for the vet to dispose of.

All of these options should be discussed frankly and openly with your veterinary surgeon. Do not be afraid to ask financial questions. Cremations can be individual, but a less expensive option is mass cremation, although of course the ashes can not then be returned. Vets can usually arrange cremation services on your behalf, but you must be aware that in Britain if your dog has died at the surgery the vet cannot legally allow you to take your dog's body home.

GETTING ANOTHER DOG?

The grief of losing your beloved dog will be as lasting as the grief of losing a human friend or relative. You cannot go out and buy another grandfather, but you can go out and buy another Bichon Frise. In most cases, if your dog died of old age (if there is such a thing), it had slowed down considerably. Do you want a new Bichon puppy to replace it? Or are you better off in finding a more mature Bichon, say two to three years of age, which will usually be housetrained and will have an already developed personality. In this case, you can find out if you like each other after a few hours of being together.

The decision is, of course, your own. Do you want another Bichon Frise or perhaps a different breed so as to avoid comparison with your beloved friend? Most people usually buy the same breed because they know (and love) the characteristics of that breed. Then, too, they often know people who have the same breed and perhaps they are lucky enough that one of their friends expects a litter soon. What could be better?

Showing Your
BICHON FRISE

When you purchased your Bichon Frise you will have made it clear to the breeder whether you wanted one just as a loveable companion and pet, or if you hoped to be buying a Bichon Frise with show prospects. No reputable breeder will have sold you a young puppy saying that it was definitely of show quality for so much can go wrong during the early weeks and months of a puppy's development. If you plan to show what you will hopefully have acquired is a puppy with 'show potential.'

To the novice, exhibiting a Bichon Frise in the show ring may look easy but it usually takes a lot of hard work and devotion to do top winning at a show such as the prestigious Crufts, not to mention a little luck too!

The first concept that the canine novice learns when watching a dog show is that each breed first competes against members of its own breed. Once the judge has selected the best member of each breed, provided that the show is judged on a Group system, that chosen dog will compete with other dogs in its group. Finally the best of each group will compete for Best in Show and Reserve Best in Show.

The second concept that you must understand is that the dogs are not actually being compared to one another. The judge compares each dog against the breed standard, which is a written descrip-

tion of the ideal specimen of the breed. Whilst some early breed standards were indeed based on specific dogs that were famous or popular, many dedicated enthusiasts say that a perfect specimen, described in the standard, has never been bred. Thus the 'perfect' dog never walked into a show ring, has never been bred and, to the woe of dog breeders around the globe, does not exist. Breeders attempt to get as close to this ideal as possible, with every litter, but

Sometimes young people find great success and fun in handling their Bichons Frises on the show circuit. Dog showing and training is a very healthy outlet for juvenile exuberance.

149

theoretically the 'perfect' dog is so elusive that it is impossible. (And if the 'perfect' dog were born, breeders and judges would never agree that it was indeed 'perfect.')

If you are interested in exploring dog shows, your best bet is to join your local breed club. These clubs often host both Championship and Open Shows, and sometimes Match meetings and Special Events, all of which could be of interest, even if you are only an onlooker. Clubs also send out newsletters and some organise training days and seminars in order that people may learn more about their chosen breed. To locate the nearest breed club for you, contact The Kennel Club, the ruling body for the British dog world. The Kennel Club governs not only conformation shows but also working trials, obedience trials, agility trials and field trials. The Kennel Club furnishes the

rules and regulations for all these events plus general dog registration and other basic requirements of dog ownership. Its annual show called the Crufts Dogs Show, held in Birmingham, is the largest bench show in England. Every year over 20,000 of the U.K.'s best dogs qualify to participate in this marvellous show which lasts four days.

The Kennel Club governs many different kinds of shows in Great Britain, Australia, South Africa and beyond. At the most competitive and prestigious of these shows, the Championship Shows, a dog can earn Challenge Certificates, and thereby become a Show Champion or a Champion. A dog must earn three Challenge Certificates under three different judges to earn the prefix of 'Sh Ch' or 'Ch.' Note that some breeds must also qualify in a field trial in order to gain the title of full champion. Challenge Certificates are awarded to a very small percentage of the dogs competing, especially as dogs which are already Champions compete with others for these coveted CCs. The number of Challenge Certificates awarded in any one year is based upon the total number of dogs in

championships ever more difficult to accomplish.

Open Shows are generally less competitive and are frequently used as 'practice shows' for young dogs. There are hundreds of Open Shows each year that can be invitingly social events and are great first show experiences for the novice. Even if you're considering just watching a show to wet your paws, an Open Show is a great choice.

Whilst Championship and Open Shows are most important for the beginner to understand, there are other types of shows in which the interested dog owner can participate. Training clubs sponsor Matches that can be

There are many types of conformation shows. Breed shows, for example, are limited to competition between dogs of the same breed.

The winner and his trophies! Even the dog seems to be smiling about his successful day in the ring.

each breed entered for competition. There three types of Championship Shows, an all-breed General Championship show for all Kennel-Club-recognised breeds; a Group Championship Show, limited to breeds within one of the Groups; and a Breed Show, usually confined to a single breed. The Kennel Club determines which breeds at which Championship Shows will have the opportunity to earn Challenge Certificates (or tickets). Serious exhibitors often will opt not to participate if the tickets are withheld at a particular show. This policy makes earning

entered on the day of the show for a nominal fee. In these introductory-level exhibitions, two dogs are pulled out of a hat and 'matched,' the winner of that match goes on to the next round, and eventually only one dog is left undefeated.

Exemption Shows are much more light-hearted affairs with usually only four pedigree classes and several 'fun' classes, all of which can be entered on the day. The proceeds of an Exemption Show must be given to a charity and are sometimes held in conjunction with small agricultural shows. Limited Shows are also available in small number, but entry is restricted to members of the club which hosts the show, although one can usually join the club when making an entry.

Before you actually step into the ring, you would be well advised to sit back and observe

Behind the scenes at the Bichon benches during the prestigious Crufts Dog Show. There is a flurry of activity as the dogs are groomed to perfection before being presented in the ring.

the judge's ring procedure. If it is your first time in the ring, do not be over-anxious and run to the front of the line. It is much better to stand back and study how the exhibitor in front of you is performing. The judge asks each handler to 'stand' the dog, hopefully showing the dog off to his best advantage. The judge will observe the dog from a distance and from different angles, approach the dog, check his teeth, overall structure, alertness and muscle tone, as well as consider how well the dog 'conforms' to the standard. Most importantly, the judge will have the exhibitor move the dog around the ring in some pattern that he or she should specify (another advantage to not going first, but always listen since some judges change their directions, and the judge is always right!). Finally the judge will give the dog one last look before moving on to the next exhibitor.

If you are not in the top three at your first show, do not be discouraged. Be patient and consistent and you may eventually find yourself in the winning lineup. Remember that the winners were once in your shoes and have devoted many hours and much money to earn the placement. If you find that your dog is losing every time and never getting a nod, it may be time to consider a different dog sport or just enjoy your Bichon Frise as a pet.

WORKING TRIALS

Working trials can be entered by any well-trained dog of any breed, not just Gundogs or Working dogs. Many dogs that earn the Kennel Club Good Citizen Dog award choose to participate in a working trial. There are five stakes at both open and championship levels: Companion Dog (CD), Utility Dog (UD), Working Dog (WD), Tracking Dog (TD) and Patrol Dog (PD). As in conformation shows, dogs compete against a standard and if the dog reaches the qualifying mark, it obtains a certificate. Divided into groups, each exercise must be achieved 70 percent in order to qualify. If the dog achieves 80 percent in the open level, it receives a Certificate of Merit (COM), in the championship level, it receives a Qualifying Certificate. At the CD stake, dogs must participate in four groups, Control, Stay, Agility and Search (Retrieve and Nosework). At the next three levels, UD, WD and TD, there are only three groups: Control, Agility and Nosework.

Agility consists of three jumps: a vertical scale up a wall of planks; a clear jump over a basic hurdle with a removable top bar; and a long jump across angled planks.

To earn the UD, WD and TD, dogs must track approximately one-half mile for articles laid

Participating in dog shows can be a wonderful experience for dog and owner. If you have a good quality Bichon Frise, do not be afraid to have it evaluated for showing.

from one-half hour to three hours ago. Tracks consist of turns and legs, and fresh ground is used for each participant.

The fifth stake, PD, involves teaching manwork, which is not recommended for every breed.

AGILITY TRIALS
Agility trials began in the United Kingdom in 1977 and have since spread around the world, especially to the United States, where it enjoys strong popularity. The handler directs his dog over an obstacle course that includes jumps (such as those used in the working trials), as well as tyres, the dog walk, weave poles, pipe tunnels, collapsed tunnels, etc. The Kennel Club requires that dogs not be trained for agility until they are 12 months old. This dog sport intends to be great fun for dog and owner and interested owners should join a training club that has obstacles and experienced agility handlers who can introduce you and your dog to the 'ropes' (and tyres, tunnels and so on).

Bichons Frises may look like lapdogs, but actually they are quite athletic and easily can do well in agility trials if they have been trained to do so.

FÉDÉRATION CYNOLOGIQUE INTERNATIONALE

Established in 1911, the Fédération Cynologique Internationale (FCI) represents the 'world kennel club.' This international body brings uniformity to the breeding, judging and showing of purebred dogs. Although the FCI originally included only four European nations: France, Holland, Austria and Belgium (which remains its headquarters), the organisation today embraces nations on six continents and recognises well over 300 breeds of purebred dog. There are three titles attainable through the FCI: the International Champion, which is the most prestigious; the International Beauty Champion, which is based on aptitude certificates in different countries; and the International Trial Champion, which is based on achievement in obedience trials in different countries. Quarantine laws in England and Australia prohibit most of their exhibitors from entering FCI shows. The rest of the Continent does participate in these impressive canine spectacles, the largest of which is the World Dog Show,

hosted in a different country each year. FCI sponsors both national and international shows. The hosting country determines the judging system and breed standards are always based on the breed's country of origin.

A wonderful combination of personality and beauty, the Bichon Frise is truly a 'winner.'

155

Acrodermatitis 119
Adult diets 67
Age 91
Ageing signs 145
Agility trials 109, 153-154
Airlines 83
Allergies, airborne 120
American Kennel Club 13, 18, 32
—recognition 20
Anaemia 133, 137
Ancylostoma caninum **133, 135**
Ascaris lumbricoides **133**
Axelrod, Dr Herbert R 129
Azelia Gascoigne 19
Balearic Islands 9
Barbet 9
Barbichon 9
Bathing 74
Beauchamp, Richard 20
Bedding 48
Bellotte, M et Mme 17
Bichon à Poil Frisé 9
Bichon Bolognaise 9
Bichon family 9
Bichon Frise Club of America 19
Bichon Havanais 9, 12
Bichon Maltais 9
Bichon Teneriffe 9, 11, 15
Bladder Stones 28
Blanquito de la Habana 13
Boarding 84
Bolognese 9, 11
Bones 51
Bouctovagniez, Mme 16
Bowls 51
Breed name 17
Breeder 40
Britain 20
—first litter 21
Buffon 13
Burial 148
Canary Islands 9
Carlise Cicero of Tresilva 21
Cars 81

Cat 100
Cat flea 122
Cataracts 30
CDS 141
Challenge Certificates 150
Champion 150
Championship Shows 150
Charles IV 11
Chewing 95
Children 26
Choke collars 51
Coat 22, 25, 71
—care 70
—presentation 25
—texture 25
Cognitive dysfunction syndrome 141
Collar 51, 100
Colostrum 65
Colour 25, 32
Comb 73
Come 104
Commands 101
Conjunctivitis 31
Coronavirus 117
Coton de Reunion 15
Coton de Tulear 15
Crate 46, 63, 81, 94, 96
Crate training 96
Crufts Dogs Show 150
Crying 63
Ctenocephalides canis **122**
Ctenocephalides felis **122**
Cuba 13
Defleaing the house 123
Dentition 37
Dermacentor variabilis **126, 131**
Destructive behaviour 144
Development schedule 91
Deworming programme 133
Diet, puppy 65
Diet 64
—adults 67
—puppy 65
—seniors 67
Dirofilaria immitis **138**

Discipline 98
Distemper 117
Documentation 43
Dog flea 122
Dog tick 131
Down 102
Drying 74, 78
Ear cleaning 79
Ear mites 128
Ears 31
Echinococcus multilocularis **137**
Elbow dysplasia 139
Euthanasia 147
Exemption Shows 152
Exercise 69
External parasites 122
Eye problems 29
Family introduction to pup 56
FCI 16, 155
Fear period 60
Fédération Cynologique Internationale 16, 155
Fence 55
First aid 113
Fleas 122, 136
—life cycle 127
Food 64
—allergy 120
—intolerance 121
—treats 108
Fournier, Mrs 19
France 11
Francis I 11
French Revolution 12
Friends of the Belgian Breeds 16
Good Citizen Dog award 153
Goya 11
Grooming 70
Gums 29
Haloes 25
Handling 152
Havana Silk Dog 13
Havanese 9, 12

Head 23
Health 26
Heartworms 137, 138
Heel 106
Height 37
Henry III 11
Hepatitis 117
Hiking 109
Hip dysplasia 139-140
Home preparation 45
Hookworm 133, 135
Hookworm larva 136
Housebreaking 90
—schedule 97
Identification 85
Inbreeding 17
Internal parasites 128
Italy 11
Ivermectin 126, 128
Ixode 131
Jenny-Vive de Carlise 21
Judge 152
Kennel Club 21, 32, 40, 150
—registrations 23
Kennel cough 116-117
Lead 51, 100
Leptospirosis 117
Leemans, Mme Nizet de 16-17
Life expectancy 22, 142
Limited Shows 152
Line-brushing 72
Little Lion Dog 13-14
Livre des Origines
  Francaises 17
Louis XIV 11
Löwchen 14
Lupus 120
Luxating patella 28
Lyme disease 126, 131
Madagascar 15
Maltese 9, 13
Mange 128
Matches 151
Mediterranean region 9
Milk 66
Milton prefix 17

Mites 79, 126
Mosquitoes 137
Nail clipping 79
Napoleon III 12
Neutering 117
Nipping 62
Obedience class 86, 108
Obesity 69, 144
Old dog syndrome 141
Open shows 151
Ownership 43
Parasites 119
—external 122
—internal 128
Parvovirus 117
Personality 24
Petit Chien Lion 14
Picault, Helene and Francais
  18
Pigmentation 37
Pollen allergy 120
Popularity 23
Punishment 99
Puppy
—food 65
—health 112
—problems 58, 62
—training 39, 87
Puppy-proofing your home
  54
Rabies 117
Rava's Regal Valor
  of Reenroy 21
Reunion 15
Rhabditis 134, 135
Rocky Mountain spotted
  fever 126
Roundworms 129, 133-135
Sabella, Frank 20
Scissoring 78
Selecting a puppy 42
Senior 142
—diets 67
Separation anxiety 63, 144
Shampoo 74
Show Champion 150
Sit 102

Skin allergies 28
Skin problems 118
—inherited 118
Socialisation 58
Sorstein, J 21
Spain 9
Standard 149
Stay 103
Tapeworms 133, 136
Tear staining 23, 31
Teeth 29, 37
Teneriffe 9
Thorndike, Dr Edward 99
Thorndike's Theory of
  Learning 99
Tickets 151
Ticks 126
Toxocara canis 129
Toy Club of France 16
Toys 49
Tracheobronchitis 116
Training 62
—equipment 100
—puppy 39, 87
Travelling 81
Treats 100
Tresilva Don Azur 21
Trimming 37
Umbilical hernias 42
Undercoat 26, 32
Urine sample 27
USA 18
Vaccinations 114
Veterinary surgeon 56, 111,
  118, 125, 133, 139
Water 69
Weight 23, 26
Whining 63
Working trials 153

My Bichon Frise

PUT YOUR PUPPY'S FIRST PICTURE HERE

Dog's Name _____

Date _____ Photographer _____